Table of Contents:

Compiled בעזרהי'ת by Rabbi Yisroel M. Ungar
Comments are welcome. 917.692.6394
Ymungar@gmail.com

הסכמות ודברי ברכה

INTRODUCTION

CHAPTER I

הלכות ברכות

CHAPTER I – הלכות ברכות
INTRODUCTION

1. The גמרא says it is אסור to eat any food without first making a ברכה, and if one does so, it is considered stealing. The גמרא continues: Therefore, it is incumbent on each of us to make sure we are proficient in the הלכות of making ברכות. (ברכות לה.)

2. The גמרא says that if you eat without first making a ברכה it is as if you stole from הקב'ה and from כלל ישראל. It is as if you stole from 'ה because it is His food and חז'ל say that you cannot eat it without a ברכה. It is also stealing from כלל ישראל because every time you make a ברכה you bring ברכה into the world, and by not making a ברכה you are stealing that ברכה from the world. (ברכות לה:)

3. The ריטב'א (הלכות ברכות פרק ראשון אות א'), after quoting the many exhortations of חז'ל that say how terrible it is to eat without a ברכה, says, "Therefore, it is fitting for every person, that the FIRST THING to teach children and students is הלכות ברכות, so that they do not come to this terrible act of stealing from 'ה and of all the other descriptions of חז'ל about one who eats without a ברכה!" We must learn it as children and, even more importantly, as adults so that we can follow the הלכות properly.

4. A ברכה is an opportune time to really thank 'ה. When you are about to eat something, especially when you are very hungry, and you stop and think and make a ברכה properly, you are showing 'ה that even though you are in a rush to eat you are still not forgetting to first say thank-you. The more כוונה you have, the greater the show of thanks it is to 'ה. You are showing that no matter what, you are acknowledging that everything is from 'ה and that you would not have anything without Him. This is a way of showing yourself and anyone around you that 'ה runs the world and that everything belongs to Him and comes from Him. 'ה is hidden from us, and without thinking we will not realize that it is He who gives us everything we have, so we need to work on ourselves to give הכרת הטוב, which can be greatly accomplished through our ברכות.

5. An עצה that the חפץ חיים gives for one who is *davening*, and especially in שמונה עשרה, is to *daven* from a Siddur. Looking inside definitely

helps one's concentration. A second עצה he gives for שמונה עשרה is: before each ברכה, pause for two seconds and think about the ברכה you are about to say. That will help you concentrate on the ברכה. This עצה can be very helpful for every ברכה you make on food. Think for a second that you are about to say thank-you to 'ה for the delicious food, and that will help you have כוונה.

6. A few things to know about all ברכות are:

   a. Every ברכה was made up by עזרא ובית דינו and one is not allowed to change the נוסח. (רמב'ם ברכות פ'א ה'ה)

   b. Every ברכה has hidden meanings to which we are not privy. (כי (החיים קפז', ד' – שם מדובר על ברכת המזון ובזאת הברכה ל' שפשוט שה'ה בענין ברכות

   c. Just like תפלה, a ברכה has a specific purpose in this world and when it is said properly, it breaks through the שמים and goes straight to 'ה. (נפש החיים שער ב' פרק י')

   d. When you say a ברכה to the best of your ability even without having all the proper כוונות that חז'ל had in mind when creating the ברכה, it is as if you had all those כוונות. (יסוד שורש ועבודה שער הברכות פ'י)

   e. The main כוונה to have is to thank 'ה for doing חסד with you in giving you this food to eat and enjoy. The גמרא says that when making a ברכה, you should not just throw it out of your mouth but rather say it בנחת. (משנה ברורה ס' ה' ס'ק א')

7. When making a ברכה, you should לכתחלה hear the words coming out of your mouth. בדיעבד if you didn't hear the words (for example, there was a lot of noise in the room) you are יוצא as long as you said the words. Merely thinking the words is not a ברכה. (קפה' סעי' ב' ומ'ב ס'ק ב')

8. The חפץ חיים says that it is a good idea to say a ברכה loudly, as it helps you have כוונה. (מ'ב קפה' ס'ק ג')

9. **ברוך אתה י - ה - ו - ה אלוקינו מלך העולם:**

   a. When saying the word ברוך, one should have in mind that 'ה is the מקור of all ברכה in the world, that 'ה created the world to be מטיב to all His creations, and that He should give us this goodness. By making a ברכה we enable ourselves to accept all the טוב that 'ה wants to give us. (ע'י בספר וזאת הברכה במאמר ד' בביאור מילות הברכה)

b. When saying **אתה** one should have in mind the simple meaning "You." Question: How are we allowed to talk to 'ה like a friend and say, "You?" It seems very disrespectful. The answer is: 'ה wants us to talk to Him like a friend so that we will talk to Him more and more, and so that we should feel that we can ask anything of Him. 'ה really enjoys when we have a close relationship with Him.

c. When saying **ה - ו - ה - י** which is pronounced 'א' ד' נ' י, one should have in mind that 'ה is the אדון הכל, that everything depends solely on Him, and that all existence is through 'ה's word. Some say to also have in mind שהוא היה הוה ויהיה. (א' סעי' ה' סימן
ג' ס'ק שם מ'ב ע' -)

d. One should make sure to say the 'א with a חטף פתח, the 'ד with a חולם, the 'נ with a קמץ, to hear the 'י at the end, and it should be said מלרע; meaning, the accent of the word should be on the end of the word on the 'נ.

e. When saying **אלוקינו** you should have in mind our G-d Who has the strength to take care of the entire universe. (שם)

f. When saying **מלך העולם** we are saying that 'ה is the One Who rules the world and that everything we do is for His כבוד, as we know כל מה שברא הקב'ה בעולמו לא ברא אלא לכבודו. (אבות ו', י'א)

10. When we say ברכות on food we say בורא מיני מזונות or בורא פרי העץ or והאדמה. We use the present tense of בורא. Why don't we say ברא in לשון עבר—past tense—since the food we are eating was already created? This teaches us an important lesson in אמונה. 'ה is מחדש בכל יום תמיד and if 'ה would take away His השגחה even for a split second, the entire universe would fall apart and we would cease to exist. The apple you are about to eat is only there because 'ה is right now seeing to it that it is there. (ערוך השלחן סי' קס'ז סעי' ז')

11. Another important point to bear in mind when making ברכות or by any תפלה is to make sure to say the words clearly, without

swallowing the words. If you swallow a word, that means you did not say that word even if you are thinking about that word. (כף החיים סי' ה' אות ב')

12. Most people do not realize how much their תפילות make a difference. The יסוד ושורש העבודה, who was a צדיק וקדוש from 300 years ago and who was a contemporary of the גר'א, says that you should be extra careful to put space between all words in all your תפילות, and even when learning תנ'ך. He writes: A certain חסיד testified that he heard from אליהו הנביא that the reason why this גלות is so long is because we are not careful while *davening* to say the words correctly. He doesn't say it's because we don't have proper כוונה, but rather because we don't say the words properly. He continues and says that every word in *davening* accomplishes a תיקון גדול in שמים in the עולמות העליונים. If a person does not say the words correctly, he is missing out on this very vital accomplishment. If one swallows a word or says only half a word, that word is not considered a word and cannot do what it has to do. Over and over, he stresses this point that the most important part of *davening* is to say the words correctly. The נפש החיים says that you are יוצא *davening* even if you do not know the meaning of the words as long as you did say the words. We are not holding by understanding all the proper כוונות in all the words. However, we definitely are capable of saying the words slowly, so that they come out whole and not half-eaten. This is all true in regard to ברכות as well.

13. כוונה/concentration: If you space out during *davening* or ברכות, it is a very low מדרגה of תפלה, and perhaps some would say that it is as if you didn't really *daven*. (עי' משנ'ב סי' ה' ס'ק א' ומנחת שלמה ח'א סי' א' אות ב') We said earlier that even without כוונה one is יוצא, but that is if you at least realize that you are talking to ה'. If you're thinking about destinations for your upcoming vacation, perhaps you are not יוצא. In the event that you find yourself spacing out, the trick is not to despair, but to try at that moment to make the best of the remaining *davening* or ברכה. If you're up to רפאנו in שמונה עשרה and don't recall too much of what you said until that point, just continue on with the mindset that you will try to concentrate for the rest of your שמונה עשרה. Do your best.

14. **אמן:** The גמרא says that one who answers אמן accomplishes something greater than the one who makes a ברכה. The ספר חסידים explains: One who makes a ברכה only mentions 'ה's name once, however, one who answers אמן mentions 'ה's name twice, as the גימטריא of אמן is that of 'ה ,'ו ,'ה ,'י and of 'י ,'נ ,'ד ,'א. (ברכות נג: ספר חסידים סעי' יח')

15. Following are some הלכות pertaining to the answering of אמן:

    a. One is obligated to answer אמן to every ברכה that one hears. (סימן קכד' סעי' ו' –סימן רטו' סעי' ב')

    b. Even if you hear someone giving a ברכה without 'ה's name, you also are supposed to say אמן. For example, if one says ברוך רופא חולים, "You should have a רפואה שלימה," "You should become a ירא שמים," etc., one should answer אמן. (סי' רטו' מ'ב ס'ק ט')

    c. When saying אמן one should be מיכוין that what you're hearing is אמת and that you believe it. (סי' קכד' סעי' ו')

    d. When answering אמן you should not say it louder than the מברך unless it is for the purpose to get others to answer too. (סימן קכד' סעי' יב' מ'ב ס'ק מז')

    e. There are three types of אמן's that are אסור to answer:

       1. **אמן חטופה** – To say אמן before the מברך finishes. (שם סעי' ח')

       2. **אמן קטופה** – To say אמן that is cut-off, meaning you swallow the 'א or 'נ. (שם)

       3. **אמן יתומה** – To answer an אמן that has no parents, meaning, it has nothing to attach itself to, meaning:(שם)

          • If you answer late, after תוך כדי דיבור. (מ'ב שם ס'ק לד')

          • If you answer אמן and you have no idea what the ברכה was. (Meaning, you don't have to actually hear the ברכה, but you have to at least know what the ברכה was, and then you are allowed to answer אמן, but only if you don't need that ברכה for yourself. For example, if someone is making a העץ on an apple, you can answer אמן even if you didn't hear the ברכה as long as you saw he was eating an apple. But if you just hear others answering אמן, you may not answer with them.)

          • If you answer אמן to a ברכה that you need to be יוצא with (like קידוש or מגילה) and you missed a part of the ברכה that makes a difference like 'ה's name or עיקר words of the ברכה. (ביאור הלכה סעי' ח' ד'ה וזה)

    f. Lastly, the גמרא (שם מז.) says harsh things for answering any of these three אמן's, so one should be very careful with all these הלכות.

שינוי מקום

CHAPTER II

הלכות ברכות

1. **שינוי מקום:** If you finished eating a food and you made a ברכה אחרונה on it, you will need to make a new ברכה ראשונה if you want more of that food. Even if you did not yet make a ברכה אחרונה and you still want to eat more, but you left your original eating place, there are times you will need a new ברכה before continuing to eat. (סי' קעח' סעי' א')

2. If one makes a ברכה on a food/drink that requires a בורא נפשות and then makes a שינוי מקום, a new ברכה is required to be allowed to continue eating/drinking. This is true whether you wish to continue eating in your new location, or even if you go back to your original location. The words "שינוי מקום" mean "change of location." When you leave your original eating place, it is as if you are saying you are finished eating and, therefore, you need a new ברכה. (שם במ'ב ס'ק ו')

3. For example: If you were eating potato chips, an apple, or sipping a hot cocoa and went outside, you need a new ברכה to continue eating since you have made a שינוי מקום.

4. The הלכות of שינוי מקום **do not** apply to:
   a. פת (רמ'א סי' קעח' סעי' ב', וה')
   b. מזונות that requires על המחיה (If you ate a כזית, see #5) (רמ'א שם סעי' ה')
   c. שבעת המינים (בדיעבד -see #6) (שם ומ'ב ס'ק מה')
   d. If you eat with others.

(The reason: The הלכה is that if you left your place of eating before making a ברכה אחרונה, for בורא נפשות you do not have to go back to make it and you can make it wherever you are. However, if you need ברכת המזון or על המחיה/הגפן/העץ, then ideally you need to return to your original place of eating to make that ברכה אחרונה. What follows is: If you do not have to return to make the ברכה אחרונה, we look at it as if you are finished eating, and that is called a שינוי מקום, which requires you to make a new ברכה if you want to eat more. If, however, you are still required to return to make the ברכה אחרונה, then we look at it as if you still are not finished; that is why it is not considered a שינוי מקום and you can eat more without a new ברכה.)

5. **פת/מזונות:** Based on the above, if you were eating bread or cookies and you went outside, when you want to continue eating, either outside or when you come back in, you do not need a new ברכה. However, this is only true if you already had at least a כזית of bread or cookie. For example, if you washed and only nibbled a drop and then ran outside, you will need a new המוציא. (סי' קעח' מ'ב ס'ק כח')

12

6. **שבעת המינים:** Regarding the שבעת המינים, since some hold that it is not like פת and מזונות, one should avoid the שאלה and make sure not to leave in the middle of eating or drinking wine. If you did leave and you want to continue eating, you may do so without a new ברכה. (על פי המ'ב)

שם ס'ק מה' ועי' וזאת הברכה פרק ו' דף 60 אות ג')

7. **Eating together with another:** If you were eating together with at least one other person, and after leaving the house and coming back (which was your plan) that person is still there, you will not need to make a new ברכה to continue eating. Since your "partner" is still there, it is as if the partner was holding on to your ברכה for you; it is as if you never left. (רמ'א סי' קעח' סעי' ב' ומ'ב ס'ק כז')

8. **על המחיה/בורא נפשות:** If you were eating two foods, one that requires על המחיה and one that requires בורא נפשות, and you left your מקום, for the על המחיה food you do not need a new ברכה no matter the case, but as far as the בורא נפשות food goes, it depends if you come back or not:

   a. If you come back to your original place where you made your ברכה, then you do not have to make a new ברכה. (קצות השלחן סי' נז' ס'ק ה')

   בבדי השלחן, פסקי תשובות סי' קעח' אות עג' ד'ה אבל וכו', ובצירוף שיטת אג'מ או'ח ה' סי' טז' אות י' אע'פ שהוא חידש הלכה בענין (שינוי מקום שלא קיבלו הפוסקים

   b. If you do not go back to your original place, it is unclear if you should/could make a new ברכה (עי' שלמי ברכה פרק פ' דף תקצא' ד'ה שותה שהביא בשם ר') ש.ז.א. שמסופק בזה) and it is therefore better not to continue eating, or you can make a ברכה on a different food. If you don't have any other food and you need to continue eating, then you should make a new ברכה. (קצות השלחן שם, פסקי תשובות שם, וזאת הברכה פרק ו' דף 60 אות ו' בשם ר' אלישב)

9. We have established that all the הלכות of שינוי מקום that we will discuss **only** apply to foods on which you make a בורא נפשות, including rice (even though it is a מזונות) and only if you were eating alone.

10. The rules of שינוי מקום apply and you will need a new ברכה:

    a. Even if you have in mind (when making the ברכה) to leave that place and/or come back. (סי' קעח' רמ'א סעי' א' – "בבית אחד")

    b. Even if you go back to the original place where you started eating. (מחבר שם)

    c. Even if you leave only for a moment. (שם במ'ב ס'ק ב')

11. A שינוי מקום must be a halachic change of location. If you leave the building you were in, it is considered a halachic שינוי מקום unless you can still see the original place where you started eating. (See #23-24)

12. For example: If you were eating an apple in your house and walked outside to talk to a friend, you will need a new ברכה when you want to continue eating that apple. Leaving your house is a halachic שינוי מקום. (מחבר קע"ח, א')

13. Another example: If you leave your house while drinking a coffee and start walking or driving to yeshiva or school, you will need a new ברכה to continue drinking, unless you are a traveler. (See #30)

14. **UNDER ONE ROOF:** If you move around within your house or a building that is owned by one person or entity, even if you go to a different room, that is not considered a שינוי מקום, and you do not need a new ברכה (since it is the דרך to move around the house). However, since some are of the opinion that moving around from room to room is indeed a שינוי מקום, one should לכתחלה have כוונה to move around when making the ברכה on that food (רמ"א קע"ח סע"י א'), but even if you didn't have it in mind you are allowed to go. (Since these days most people regularly move around while eating, it is as if one automatically has it in mind, which helps within a house.) (עי' מ"ב סי' קע"ח ס"ק י"ב' ובביאור הלכה.בסוף ד"ה בבית אחד. וזאת הברכה פ'ו דף 58 אות ב')

15. In a school, hospital or the like where the building is owned by one person or entity, it has a הלכה like your house and it is okay to roam the entire building. (לכתחלה you should have in mind to roam.)

16. **APARTMENT BUILDING/HOTEL/STAIRWELL/LOBBY:** If you go from apartment to apartment within a building or even if you go into the stairwell or lobby of a building that is owned or rented by different people there is a מחלוקת in the *poskim*. Some opine that as long as you are under one roof, if you have in mind to go from apartment to apartment you are allowed to go, and it is not considered a שינוי מקום. (ערוך השלחן סי' קע"ח סע"י י"א' אור לציון תשובות ב', טז', בצל החכמה ח'ו סי' ע') Others hold that it is the same as going from house to house and having in mind doesn't help. (וזאת הברכה דף 56 בשם כמה פוסקים) Since it is a מחלוקת, you should avoid this שאלה and either:

     a.   Finish eating and then leave your apartment.

b. Make a ברכה אחרונה before leaving your apartment, and then you can make a new ברכה when you get to the new apartment. (It's not considered a ברכה שאינה צריכה since you need it to satisfy the opinions that consider it a שינוי מקום)

c. Go outside the building to make a real שינוי מקום which will then allow you to make a new ברכה.

d. Find a different food to make a ברכה on.

e. Listen to someone else's ברכה.

17. If you are already in the stairwell or different apartment and want to continue eating, you should choose one of the last 3 options in #16. (Making a new ברכה is a שאלה of a ברכה לבטלה and the rule is ספק ברכה להקל. So, if you cannot do any of the above options, and you must continue eating, then you should do so without a new ברכה.)

18. **HAVING IN MIND:** In #10.a we said that having in mind does not help, but there is a situation where it does help—in a park or camp that is not enclosed, if you have in mind to roam around, you can eat anywhere in the outdoor areas of the park or camp without needing a new ברכה. (The reason is since you are somewhat in the same מקום. See #21.b)

19. **ENCLOSED AREA:** If you have a bunch of houses that are **enclosed** within a gate, each house is a separate מקום, and the entire outdoor area is also considered a separate מקום. An example of this is a bungalow colony, a camp, or a complex of many houses. (סי' קעח' מ'ב ס'ק כה')

20. Based on the above:

a. If you made a ברכה in one house and walked outside, you will need a new ברכה.

b. If you were eating outside and then you walked inside to one of the houses, you will need a new ברכה.

c. If two of the houses share one roof, then it is a מחלוקת and one should avoid going. See above #16.

d. If you started eating outside, as long as you are outside within the enclosed area, you will not need a new ברכה, even if you cannot see the original place where you made your ברכה, since the entire outdoor area is considered one מקום.

21. **NON-ENCLOSED AREA**: A specific area that is **not** enclosed is considered one מקום in one of two ways:

    a. If you can still see the original place where you made your ברכה. (סי' קעח' מ'ב ס'ק כה')

    b. You had in mind to walk around that area. (שם)

22. Some examples:

    a. If you are in a park or camp that is not enclosed, and you start eating on a bench and then walk away to a spot where you <u>cannot</u> see that original bench, if you had in mind when making your ברכה to walk around, you <u>do not</u> need a new ברכה to continue eating, but if you did not have it in mind then you need to make a new ברכה. If you <u>can</u> still see the original place where you made your ברכה, then even if you did not have in mind to move, you do not need a new ברכה.

    b. If you started eating ice cream in your yard and went to your neighbor's yard (לכתחלה you should not do so), if there is no public street in between and you can still see your yard, and at no point was your view of your yard obstructed, then no new ברכה is needed. If there is a public street in between, you need a new ברכה because it is considered a totally different מקום. (וזאת הברכה דף 58 אות ה' בשם קצות השלחן סי' נז' בבדה'ש ס'ק ב')

23. **ORIGINAL מקום CAN STILL BE SEEN**: If you make a halachic שינוי מקום by leaving the building, but from outside the door the original place where you were eating can still be seen (the door is open or there is a window), you do not need to make a new ברכה. As long as you can see any part of the room where you were originally eating it is good enough. You do not have to see the table at which you were eating. (וזאת הברכה דף 58 אות א') So, if you stepped out of your house to get a package, if you can see the original room in which you ate, you will not need a new ברכה.

24. However, some say that only from room to room or in one big area that is not enclosed does seeing the original place help, but if you leave a building or any מקום and you go into a new מקום then seeing the original place doesn't help. Since this is so, you should לכתחלה

not leave a מקום even if you will be able to see your original place, but if you did go בדיעבד, or בשעת הדחק that you have to go, you can continue eating without a new ברכה. (ע'י מ'ב סי' רעג' ס'ק ז' ושער הציון אות ח')

(ע'י משנה ברורה סי' קעח' ס'ק יב' ושער הציון אות ט' שיש ספק בזה, אבל בס'ק לט' משמע שודאי לא מהני ראיית מקומו הראשון וצ'ע)

25. **ORIGINAL מקום CANNOT BE SEEN:** If at any point while outside you can't see the original room in which you were eating, you will need a new ברכה.

26. Some examples:

   a. If you walked outside and went to sit in your front lawn which is not enclosed (see end of #28), even if from your lawn you can see in through a window, if at any point from your door till your lawn your view is blocked, you will need a new ברכה.

   b. If you started an apple in your kitchen and went out your door to your neighbor's house, and you can see your kitchen through a window, you will still need a new ברכה if on your way to your neighbor there is a point that you cannot see your kitchen. If you both have sliding glass doors through which you can see from kitchen to kitchen then you won't need a new ברכה.

   c. If you went outside, to a spot where you cannot see inside, to help your mother bring in packages from the car and you were in the middle of eating a bowl of chicken soup, when you come back and want to continue eating, you will need a new ברכה. If you were in middle of eating chocolate chip cookies, you will not need a new ברכה. In all these examples, one should really not leave unless it is urgent. Going to help unload a car is a good reason to have to leave and you may do so, but you will have to apply הלכות שינוי מקום.

27. **PORCH WITH A ROOF:** If your porch is attached to your house and it has a roof over it, then all agree that it is considered part of your house. A סוכה that is attached to your house is considered like a porch with a roof, which is like another room in your house. A סוכה that is not attached to your house and is in a backyard that is not enclosed is considered a שינוי מקום. If it is in an enclosed backyard

then it has the same הלכה as a porch without a roof. See next הלכה.

(וזאת הברכה דף 56 אות ו'. הדין של סוכה – ביאור הלכה סי' רע'ג ד'ה ומבית לסוכה)

28. **PORCH WITHOUT A ROOF/ENCLOSED BACKYARD:** Some say going to a porch that has no roof, even if it is attached to your house, is a שינוי מקום, and unless you can still see the original place where you made your ברכה you will need a new ברכה. However, others say that if you use your porch throughout the year for sitting or playing there, etc., then it is considered part of your house. One can rely on those who say that it is a part of the house; however, it is a good idea to have כוונה to go there when making your ברכה. An enclosed back or front yard has the same הלכה like this הלכה of a porch without a roof. If a backyard is <u>not</u> enclosed, then it is considered a שינוי מקום.

(שם אות ו', וז')

29. **CONTINUOUS EATING:** If you are continuously eating, then even if you go to a new place, you do not need to make a new ברכה. For example, sucking a candy or chewing gum, which is continuous eating, does not need a new ברכה. When eating a bag of potato chips or a banana there are usually breaks in between bites, so that is not considered continuous eating. If the break between bites is always less than two seconds, that is also considered continuous eating. If you are sipping an iced coffee, you take breaks, and that is not continuous eating. (אגרת משה או'ח ח'ב סי' נז')

30. **TRAVELER:** When you are traveling, you are not considered to be in any particular place. Therefore, as you go and are moving from place to place, you do not need a new ברכה, even if you didn't have it in mind and even if you can't see the original place. A שינוי מקום is when you were in one place and then left it. If you are nowhere (i.e., a traveler), then you are not changing your location. (סי' קעח' סעי' ד' ומ'ב ס'ק מב')

31. If you are planning to leave your house to go somewhere, and you are ready to leave but you are waiting for your ride or walking partner, you are already considered a traveler. So, if for example, you started a coffee in your house and you immediately left, you will not need a new ברכה when you get into the car or start walking. (אג'מ או'ח ב' סי' נז')

32. However, if you are not ready to leave for another few minutes, and you started your coffee, then when you leave your house, you will need a new ברכה. Since you were settled in your house for those few minutes, you were קובע מקום, and leaving is a שינוי מקום. (שם)

33. The same is true if you sit down in a park or mall to eat and you plan on staying for a little while. That is like you are being קובע מקום, and when you leave that place it will be considered a שינוי מקום.

34. Some examples:

   a. If you started a coffee in your car on the way to school, when you walk into school you will not need a new ברכה, since while you were traveling you were nowhere, and entering school is not a change of location.

   b. If you started eating while walking outside, even if you walk all the way to China, the original ברכה remains valid the whole trip. Even if on the way you stop at a store to buy something, your first ברכה is valid, since you did not settle into the store.

   c. If you are going walking and you have water with you that you are slowly sipping, you do not need a new ברכה the whole walking session. Even if you stop along the way for a few minutes to rest or if you went into a friend's house for a few minutes and then you continued walking, you do not need a new ברכה since you are a traveler.

   d. If you buy a coffee in a store and make a ברכה to taste it, when you leave the store you will not need a new ברכה to continue drinking, since you are a traveler.

35. **CAR:** Traveling in a car is like walking and you are not considered in a מקום. Any ברכה you make in the car remains valid the whole car trip. If you are going around doing errands, in and out of stores without staying too long, your ברכה remains valid the whole time since you are a traveler. (וזאת הברכה ור' באדנר בשם ר' אלישב זצ'ל) (I am unsure of the following scenario and one should ask a Rov if it is applicable to you: You are traveling in a car doing errands and you made a שהכל on your iced coffee, and then you went into a store, knowing you would for sure be there for a half-hour or longer. If you take your iced coffee with you and you are slowly sipping it the whole time in the store, will that become a קביעות, and then when you leave the store will you need a new ברכה?)

36. **MALL:** If you are constantly on the move, you are a traveler and you do not need a new ברכה. (See #30) If you sit down at a table or on a bench with the intention to eat lunch and then to continue on your way to shop, since you were קובע a מקום, you will need a new ברכה when you leave that מקום. If, for example, you were inside at a bench when you ate your lunch or snack, and then you went outside to shop, you will need a new ברכה. The same is true vice versa. A mall under one roof is like an apartment building (see #16 - #17), so if you settle in store to eat and then leave the store it is a מחלוקת if you need a new ברכה to continue eating, and it should be avoided.

37. **USEFUL עצה:** Rav Moshe Feinstein gives an עצה: In any case where you are unsure if you need a ברכה, you can make a real שינוי מקום by leaving the building or by going into a different building, and then you can make a new ברכה. This obviously cannot work for מזונות or שבעת המינים, and it won't work if you can still see your original מקום. There are times that one is unsure if he made a ברכה on something, in which case one can employ this עצה from R' Moshe. (אגרות משה אוח'ד סימן מ' אות א')

38. In cases where one made a ברכה but it is a מחלוקת if you are יוצא, then the הלכה is that you may continue eating. Rav Moshe will only apply to a case where you don't know if you made a ברכה at all, so in order not to eat without a ברכה you should make a שינוי מקום if possible. If you made a ברכה and it is a מחלוקת if you are יוצא then you are not eating without a ברכה if you continue eating. See Chapter VII.

שיעורים

CHAPTER III

הלכות ברכות

1. **ברכה ראשונה:** When making a ברכה ראשונה on any food there is no required amount; one makes a ברכה even on a משהו/tiny amount. (סימן ר'
סעי' א' ומ'ב ס'ק ג')

2. **ברכה אחרונה:** To be able to make a ברכת המזון or על המחיה/העץ or a בורא נפשות, one must eat a כזית worth of food. This is equal to the volume of 1 fluid ounce, which is approximately a one-ounce schnapps cup. (סי' ר'י סעי' א')

3. **כדי אכילת פרס:** Literally translated, this means: the time it takes to eat a portion. The שיעור כזית must be eaten in the כדי אכילת פרס in order to be able to make a ברכה אחרונה. (מ'ב סי' ר'י ס'ק א') There are different opinions how much time this שיעור is. The different times range between 2 and 9 minutes. One really should try to eat a שיעור within 3 minutes (אג'מ או'ח ד'
'מא), but 4 minutes is also okay. (שיעורי תורה ג', טו) If you didn't eat a כזית within 4 minutes then you should not make a ברכה אחרונה.

4. **ספק** (סי' רט' סעי' ג' – ומ'ב ס'ק ט'-י' וסימן קפד' סעי' ד' ומ'ב שם.):

   a. **BENTCHING:** If a man eats enough bread כדי שביעה (enough to fill him up—each person to his own satisfaction), and afterwards has a ספק if he *bentched*, he should preferably eat another כזית and *bentch*, but if he can't, he is allowed to and should *bentch* since it is a דאורייתא, and the rule is ספק דאורייתא לחומרא. A woman in the same predicament should preferably hear *bentching* from someone else or wash and eat another כזית and *bentch*. If those options aren't possible, she, too, may *bentch* anyway. (מ'ב בסימן קפו' ס'ק ג')

   b. **שבעת המינים:** If you ate a כדי שביעה of the שבעת המינים, and afterwards you're not sure if you made a מעין ג' of על העץ, you should eat another כזית of that food and then make the מעין ג'. If you don't have anything more to eat, you should not make the מעין ג'. (Some say a מעין ג' on the שבעת המינים is also a דאורייתא like bentching.)

   c. **ALL OTHER FOODS:** If you have a ספק if you ate the שיעור כזית of all other foods within כדי אכילת פרס (4 minutes) then you may not make any ברכה אחרונה. The rule is ספק דרבנן לקולא—meaning, all ברכות (besides ברכת המזון) are a מצוה דרבנן and if you have a ספק if you need one, you may not just make it and risk saying ה's name in vain.

5. **WASHING ON BREAD:** Although to be able to *bentch* you must eat a כזית, for one to be able to make a ברכה of נטילת ידים על on bread, one should eat at least a כביצה of the bread or matzoh. (מחבר סי' קנ"ח סעי' ב') A כביצה equals 2 כזיתים, which is approximately the volume of 2 fluid ounces. This שיעור, which is 2 כזיתים, can and should be eaten within 6–8 minutes. (That is כדי אכילת פרס multiplied by two.)

6. If one plans on eating less than a כביצה, then one should wash without making a נטילת ידים על. (מחבר קנ"ח סעי' ב' – חיי' אדם לו', ג' – קיצור שו'ע מ' ,א' - שער הציון שם אות ט') בשעת הדחק one will be allowed to make the ברכה of נטילת ידים על on less than a כביצה as long as at least a כזית was eaten. (גרא'א מובא בשער הציון סי' קנ'ח אות ט', אג'מ) (או'ח ח'ד סי' מא סוף ד'ה וגם, וזאת הברכה פרק ב' הערה 1 בשם ר' אלישב) If, for example, you washed with the plan to eat a כביצה but then you couldn't eat more because you are full or the bread doesn't taste good, then you do not have to eat more than a כזית. If, for health reasons, one cannot eat more than a כזית one should ask their Rov.

7. **LESS THAN A כזית OF BREAD:** When eating bread, if one did not eat a כזית within כדי אכילת פרס then it is questionable if all the other foods eaten during the meal are covered by the המוציא and would perhaps require a separate ברכה. The reason: Normally, all other foods eaten during a meal are טפל/secondary to the bread and are covered by the המוציא. If less than a כזית of bread was eaten, since it is such a small amount, the other foods are **not** טפל to it and, therefore, they perhaps require their own ברכה. (אג'מ או'ח ד' סי' מא')

8. Therefore, if you insist on washing and eating only less than a כזית then you should first make a ברכה on the other foods and then wash without a ברכה and then eat the bread. One should not wash on a כזית of bread with the intention just to get out of making the other ברכות. (קעז' מ'ב ס'ק ג')

9. **SIZE:** The approximate amount of bread one needs to eat to be able to make נטילת ידים על is a half of a center slice of a <u>large</u> bakery rye bread. This equals a כביצה. The amount of matzoh needed to be able to make נטילת ידים על is 8/10 of a machine matzoh. (Kizayis book by R' Bodner page 86-87)

10. **DRINKS:** To be allowed to make a בורא נפשות on a drink, one must drink a minimum of a רביעית, which is approx. (2.9 to be exact) 3 ounces. (מחבר ס'י ר'י סע'י א')

11. **מנהג העולם:** You must drink the רביעית without a הפסק, which means drinking without putting down the cup, in which the drink goes down in a few gulps. If there is a הפסק, one would not make a ברכה אחרונה. This is the מנהג העולם. When drinking hot coffee or tea, there is always a הפסק, since one cannot swallow 3 ounces in a few gulps at one time; therefore, one does not make a בורא נפשות. (מ'ב ס'י ר'י ס'ק א' – ע'י) (הגדת קול דודי סימן ב')

12. However, the משנה ברורה says that when drinking a hot drink, it is proper to leave over a רביעית that is cool enough to drink without a הפסק, and to make בורא נפשות on it. (שם) If you insist on drinking your drink only when it's hot, then you do not have to wait till it cools off, but you should not make a בורא נפשות.

13. Some say that one is allowed to make a בורא נפשות on a drink as long as he drank the 3 ounces בכדי אכילת פרס, which means within 4 minutes. The מנהג is not this way, but one who follows this has what to rely on. (וזאת הברכה pg. 40)

14. Based on the מנהג: If you are sipping water, a very cold drink, or hot soup, and taking breaks in between the sips and you do not drink 3 ounces without a הפסק, you do not make a בורא נפשות. Generally speaking, when drinking a drink with a straw, you will also not end up drinking 3 ounces in the required timeframe.

15. **WINE:** The following are the הלכות of wine/grape juice:
    a. When one makes a ברכה on wine, that ברכה exempts all other drinks. (ס'י קעד' סע'י ב')
    b. However, for this to be true:
        i. You must drink a מלא לוגמיו/cheek-full of wine, which is approximately 2 ounces. (ביאור הלכה ס'י קעד' ס'ב ד'ה יין)
        ii. When making the ברכה, you must have כוונה to drink the other drink, or it has to be out on the table. (מ'ב שם ס'ק ג')

c. To be able to make על הגפן you must drink a רביעית. (ר"י סעי' א')

d. The same way the ברכה ראשונה exempts other drinks, the על הגפן covers other drinks. So, if you drank a רביעית of wine in a few gulps, and then a רביעית of orange juice, when you make על הגפן, that covers the orange juice and you do not need to make a בורא נפשות. (סי' רח' סעי' טז')

e. שבת morning, when hearing קידוש, one is supposed to take some wine. If you drink a מלא לוגמיו and you want to drink a coffee afterwards you don't need to make a שהכל. If you drank less than a מלא לוגמיו of wine then it is a ספק if you need a ברכה, and therefore you would need to make a שהכל on a different food while having כוונה to also drink. If you didn't drink any wine after קידוש then you are allowed to make a שהכל on a drink. (ביאור הלכה סי' קעד' ד"ה יין פוטר וכו')

16. Regarding ice cream, frozen yogurt, ices, or anything that was once liquid and then became solid, it's a מחלוקת whether it is halachically a solid or a liquid. If it is a solid, then if you eat a כזית of it within 4 minutes you can make a בורא נפשות, but if it is a liquid then you can only make a בורא נפשות if you eat 3 ounces without a הפסק like by drinking, which is impossible. Since it's a ספק, the rule is ספק ברכות לקולא and no בורא נפשות is made. (זאת הברכה page 43 וכן פסק ר' הלל דוד שליט"א) The best would be to eat or drink something else and then make a בורא נפשות.

17. Melted ice cream, yogurt, or ices is a liquid. (פשוט)

18. Fruit or anything that you blend into a liquid that has no pieces is considered a liquid, and the שיעור for a ברכה אחרונה is a רביעית. Smoothies with no pieces are a שהכל, and if you drink a רביעית in one shot it is a בורא נפשות. (רמ"א סי' רב' סעי' ז')

19. **COMBINING SIMILAR ברכות אחרונות:** All <u>**foods**</u> that have the <u>same</u> ברכה אחרונה can be מצטרף (combined) for the כזית needed to make a ברכה אחרונה. All <u>**drinks**</u> that have the same ברכה אחרונה can be מצטרף to the רביעית needed. However, food and drinks are not מצטרף. So, for example, if you drink half a כזית of orange juice and eat half a כזית of chocolate, you will not make a ברכה אחרונה. (סי' ר"י מ"ב ס"ק א')

20. **COMBINING DIFFERENT ברכות אחרונות:** The הלכה is as follows for foods that have different ברכות אחרונות:

    a. If one food is על העץ and one על המחיה, they are not מצטרף for על העץ or על המחיה, but they are מצטרף to make a בורא נפשות.
    (קיצור שו'ע נא', ד', שלמי ברכה פרק סח' הערה קל' בשם ר' ש.ז אוירבער ור' אלישב זצ'ל)

    b. If one food is ברכת המזון and one בורא נפשות you make a בורא נפשות
    (שם בקיצור שו'ע)

    c. If you eat half a כזית of bread and half a כזית of מזונות then you make a על המחיה. (שם)

    d. If one food is בורא נפשות and one food is על העץ or על המחיה, they are not מצטרף to make על העץ or על המחיה, but they are מצטרף to make בורא נפשות. (ר'י מ'ב ס'ק א') The rule is: A בורא נפשות, which is a more general ברכה, can be made even with a combination of other foods, but the more specific ברכה of על העץ or על המחיה can only be made if you have a full שיעור of those foods.

21. **PRACTICAL EXAMPLES:** (Based on #19 - #20)

    a. If you eat half a כזית of a pomegranate and half a כזית of a date, you make על העץ, since they are <u>both</u> foods and <u>both</u> על העץ.

    b. If you eat a third of a כזית of a tomato and two-thirds of a כזית of a banana, you make a בורא נפשות, since they are both foods and a בורא נפשות.

    c. If you eat half a כזית of מזונות cereal and half a כזית of milk, you do not make על המחיה or a בורא נפשות, because foods and drinks are not מצטרף at all. Even if you eat half a כזית of שהכל cereal and half a כזית of milk you do not make a בורא נפשות.

    d. If you eat half a כזית of grapes and half a כזית of cookies, you make a בורא נפשות.

    e. If you eat half a כזית of dates and half a כזית of chocolate, you make בורא נפשות and not על העץ.

שיעור עיכול

CHAPTER IV

הלכות ברכות

1. **שיעור עיכול:** The literal translation of שיעור עיכול is: "The time of digestion." One can only make a ברכה אחרונה as long as the שיעור עיכול has not passed. Once the food you ate has started to "halachically" digest, you cannot make the ברכה אחרונה you were supposed to make. (סימן קפד' סעי' ה') (Since it says ואכלת ושבעת וברכת—"And you should eat, be satisfied, and *bentch*"—once the food starts to digest and the satisfied feeling is gone, you may not *bentch* anymore.)

2. One should always make a ברכה אחרונה immediately after finishing eating for two reasons: 1. to avoid missing the chance to make one; 2. to avoid forgetting. (רמ'א סי' קעח' סעי' ב' ומ'ב ס'ק לג')

3. The שיעור עיכול starts at different times depending on what and how much you ate or drank. There are three scenarios:
   a. **Eating a large meal, enough to fill you up**
   b. **Eating a snack**
   c. **Drinking**

4. **Eating a large meal:** When you eat a large meal (made up of bread, מזונות, or any food) enough to fill you up to satisfaction, then שיעור עיכול doesn't occur until you start to feel hungry again; in this case, you are allowed to make a ברכה אחרונה as long as you are still not feeling hungry, even if it is well after 72 minutes since you last ate. Even so, לכתחלה you should still try to make your ברכה אחרונה before 72 minutes. Once you feel hungry, you lost your chance to make your ברכה אחרונה. (סי' קפד' סעי' ה' ומ'ב ס'ק כ')

5. If you are <u>unsure</u> if you are feeling hungry and it's <u>within</u> 72 minutes, you can still make your ברכה אחרונה. (שם במ'ב)

6. If you are <u>unsure</u> if you are feeling hungry and it is <u>past</u> 72 minutes since you last ate, you have a ספק on your hands and there are three options to follow:

   a. Get someone else who is making your ברכה אחרונה to be מוציא you. (וזאת הברכה פרק ה' דף 50 אות ו')

28

b. Eat another כזית of food that will require you to make the ברכה
אחרונה you need. (מ"ב ס"י קפד' ס"ק טו) If you ate bread, eat another כזית of
bread. If it is a העץ, האדמה, מזונות, or שהכל then _preferably_ you
should eat more of a _different_ type of food that requires the
same ברכה אחרונה, make a ברכה on it (something that wasn't
covered by your original ברכה), and then you can make your
needed ברכה אחרונה. If you only have some more of the same
food you were eating, eat a כזית of that and make your ברכה
אחרונה. (וזאת הברכה שם)

c. If the first two options are not feasible because no one is
around and you don't have any more food to eat, then if your
large meal was <u>bread</u>, you are allowed to *bentch*. Since you ate
a lot, which satisfied you, your חיוב to *bentch* is מן התורה; not
knowing if you still can *bentch* is a ספק דאורייתא, and the rule is
ספק דאורייתא לחומרא, and you can *bentch* even though you will
be saying 'ה's name. However, if you ate <u>other foods</u>, then your
חיוב to make a ברכה אחרונה is only a דרבנן, and in a case of a ספק
ספק ברכות you may not make a ברכה אחרונה since the rule is ספק ברכות
לקולא. (שם במ"ב קפד סי' ובערוך השלחן סי' קפד סוף סע"י ח')

7. **Eating a snack:** After eating a snack that didn't fill you up, ideally you
should make a ברכה אחרונה right away or at least before 30 minutes
elapses. After 30 minutes passed, it is a ספק if you are allowed to make
a ברכה אחרונה (כף החיים סי' קפד' כ"ט) (6) הערה 157 page-ר' אלישב) (Rabbi Bodner in name of), and you
should use options #6.a or #6.b. If those options aren't possible,
בדיעבד you can make your ברכה אחרונה up until 72 minutes.
(מ"ב קפד' ס"ק כ' וערוך השלחן סע"י ח')

(ע"י שם במ"ב קפד' ס"ק שכתב "ומ"מ אם אין לו פת יש לסמוך אסברא ראשונה ולברך ברכת המזון עד שיעור ד' מילין." משמע שיש איזה זמן, בין סוף אכילה
עד ד' מילין, דהיינו ע"ב' מינוטין, שהוא ספק אם יכול לברך וטוב לאכול כזית אחר. אלא שלא נתן אותו זמן. וע"כ כתבתי שעד חצי שעה יכול לברך בלא
העצה לאכול כזית אחר, שיכול לסמוך על הכף החיים ור' אלישב שהבאתי לעיל, ואחר חצי שעה עד ע"ב' מינוטין יש למצוא עצה כמש"כ המ"ב.)

8. **Drinks:**

a. After drinking a רביעית or more, as long as you are still satisfied
and not thirsty again, you may make a ברכה אחרונה. (סי' קפד' סע"י ה')

b. If you are unsure if you're thirsty, then within 30 minutes
you're allowed to make the ברכה אחרונה. (וזאת הברכה בשם רח.פ. שיינברג – פרק ה'
דף 51 ב.)

c. After 30 minutes have passed, you may not make a ברכה אחרונה anymore because it is a ספק, so you should either be יוצא by hearing someone else's ברכה or by drinking more. (שם- ע'י סימן קצ' מ'ב ס'ק)

(ח' שכ' ששיעור עיכול של שתיה אינו שיעור גדול כ'כ – ומשום זה לא כתבתי שיש עד ע"ב דקות אפילו בדיעבד)

d. In the summertime, when doing exercise, or when overexerting yourself with hard work, if you get thirsty very quickly, after taking a drink you should make a ברכה אחרונה right away, because once you are thirsty again you will have lost your chance to make it. Even if a short time has passed and you're very thirsty, you can't make a ברכה אחרונה anymore. (שם)

9. A LONG MEAL, SNACKING:

a. If you sit down to eat a meal, whether you washed or not, as long as you keep eating and you are in middle of your meal, the שיעור עיכול is extended, even if many hours pass. All the foods in a meal are connected. (מ'ב קפדי ס'ק יח') The "meter" starts ticking starting from your last bite of your meal.

b. Even when snacking or drinking, if you continue eating or drinking (within 72 minutes for food, and within 30 minutes for a drink.) that **same** food, then it is all connected and the שיעור עיכול ("meter") is calculated from your last bite or drink. (וזאת הברכה פרק כ' דף)

יב. 191.)

c. If, however, you are just **snacking**, and you are eating different foods, they are not connected and the שיעור עיכול for each food starts from the last bite of each particular food. (שם) So, for example, if you ate an apple and now you want a drink, both of which require a בורא נפשות, and you want to keep drinking for a while, since you are only snacking, the drink will not extend the זמן עיכול for the apple.

10. EXAMPLES OF SNACKING:

a. In the previous example, if after you finished the apple, you want to study or go walking while sipping a water bottle slowly, and you are afraid that the שיעור עיכול will pass for the apple, you should first make a בורא נפשות on the apple and then start your water bottle. After finishing your water bottle, if you drank a רביעית straight, you can make another בורא נפשות.

b. In the example of eating an apple and drinking water, if you started your water after you finished your apple and before making a בורא נפשות, and you want to continue drinking for a while but the שיעור עיכול will pass for the apple, you need to make a בורא נפשות on the apple (which will also cover the drink) and you will need a הפסק before being able to drink more, since making a new שהכל on the drink will otherwise be a ברכה שאינה צריכה. A הפסק is 30 minutes, or you can make a שינוי מקום like Rav Moshe's עצה (see Chapter II, #37). (וזאת הברכה page 52, 'ו)

c. If you want to munch on some chocolate or popcorn for a while after you drank some apple juice, your ברכה אחרונה that you need for the apple juice will expire from when you finished drinking and will not get extended by the chocolate or popcorn. (In וזאת הברכה, page 191, he says that even a piece of chocolate and a candy are considered two different things. What about a banana and an apple, or chocolate chip cookies and marble cookies? What about potato chips and corn chips? What about licorice and jelly fish? What about orange juice and milk?)

d. If you sit down to a two-hour session of schmoozing over snack, starting with cookies and then moving on to chocolate and candies, and while you're still nibbling on the chocolate, 72 minutes pass from when you finished the last bite of the cookies, you lose your על המחיה. Ideally, you should not let even 30 minutes pass.

31

ברכת המזון וברכה מעין ג'

CHAPTER V

הלכות ברכות

1. **ברכת המזון is a מצות עשה**: Before you *bentch* you should have in mind that you are about to be מקיים a מצוה דאורייתא, like it says in the תורה: ואכלת ושבעת וברכת. It is a very good idea to *bentch* from a *Siddur* and not בעל פה. (סי' קפה מ'ב ס'ק א')

2. **BREAD ON THE TABLE:** There are two reasons why there is supposed to be bread or crumbs on the table while *bentching*:
   a. It should be clear to everyone that you are thanking 'ה for the bread that you ate. (קפ' מ'ב ס'ק א')
   b. In *bentching* we are thanking 'ה and at the same time asking for ברכות, too. ברכה can only come down and attach itself to a table that has food on it and not if it is empty. (שם ס'ק ב')

3. If many people are partaking in a סעודה and they are all eating on a few different tables, every table should have bread or crumbs on it. (ח'ה קפ' ב') If there are no leftover crumbs or bread, some bread should be brought for *bentching*. (שם מ'ב ס'ק ד')

4. **BREAD IN THE GARBAGE:** There are those that say that one should not throw out bread or even crumbs straight into the garbage; rather, it should be wrapped up first, because otherwise it is a בזיון to the bread and קשה לעניות (can cause you to become poor). (קפ' סעי' ד') Some say that if the only things that are in the garbage are food items and plasticware then it is not a בזיון, and it's okay to throw bread directly in the garbage. If there are dirty diapers or the like, you should wrap the bread.

5. **MISCELLANEOUS הלכות:**
   a. If you are thirsty during your meal of bread, you should ideally drink before *bentching* so that you will have a חיוב דאורייתא of *bentching* according to all opinions. (סי' קעד מ'ב ס'ק ה')
   b. You are not allowed to talk during *bentching*. (סי' קפג סעי' ו')
   c. You should not play with anything during *bentching* that will distract you.

6. BENTCHING WHERE YOU ATE:

a. You are מחויב to *bentch* in the place that you ate. (ס"י קפד סעי' א')

b. The room in which you ate is considered your original place, even if you can't see the exact location where you ate. (שם מ"ב ס"ק א')

c. If you need to *bentch* in a different room, you can, as long as you can see the original room. (שם ס"ק א',ב')

d. If you ate in an open field or park that is not enclosed, you must *bentch* in the exact place you ate or at least within ד' אמות of it. (שם ס"ק ב' ושער הציון אות ה')

7. LEAVING BEFORE MAKING A ברכה אחרונה:

a. **לכתחלה**

b. **REASON**

c. **LEAVING ONLY FOR A MINUTE**

d. **LEAVING FOR A מצוה**

e. **EXCEPTION**

f. **LEFT WITHOUT BENTCHING**

8. **לכתחלה:** Ideally, you should not leave from the original place you started eating without making a ברכה אחרונה. (רמ"א קעח' סעי' ב' ומחבר סי' קפד' סעי' א') This applies to all foods. (שם מ"ב ס"ק ל') If you leave and you were eating פת, מזונות or שבעת המינים, you should go back and make a ברכה אחרונה. However, if you were eating anything that needs a בורא נפשות, you do not need to go back and you can just make it wherever you are.

9. **REASON:** There are two reasons for this: 1. You might forget to make a ברכה אחרונה. 2. The שיעור עיכול might pass. (שם במ"ב ס"ק לג) For example, if you drank some soda at one שלום זכור and you want to go to another one to eat and drink more, you need to make a ברכה אחרונה before you leave. When you get to the second שלום זכור you can make new ברכות there on whatever you eat or drink. (פשוט and on pg. 61 in וזאת הברכה)

10. **LEAVING FOR A MINUTE:** One may leave before *bentching* or על המחיה and בורא נפשות if the plan is to come right back. (Regarding the הלכות of שינוי מקום, see Chapter II.) However, to leave without a plan to come right back (like if you are going out to schmooze with

your neighbor for more than just a few minutes) is not allowed since you might forget to come back and *bentch*. (שער הציון סי' קעח' אות כו')

11. **LEAVING FOR A מצוה:** For a מצוה, one is allowed to leave even for more than a few minutes as long as the plan is to come back. (רמ'א סימן קעח' סוף סעי' ב' ומ'ב ס'ק לד')

12. **EXCEPTION:** There is an instance when it is מותר to leave without *bentching*. If you have in mind when you wash to eat in another house, you are allowed to leave and go there. (קעח' מ'ב ס'ק לג' וערוך השלחן סעי' ה') (REASON: Having in mind when washing to finish your meal elsewhere, you are making both places your place, and the חשש that you will forget to *bentch* does not apply. We are also not חושש that the שיעור עיכול will pass since you are going there to finish your meal.) You must eat some <u>bread</u> (קפד' מ'ב ס'ק ט') there (you don't need a כזית (מ'ב קפד' ס'ק ט') and then you can *bentch* there, or you could go back home and *bentch* at home by eating a little at home first. This is an עצה for:

    a. Someone who is in a rush and wants to finish up a meal in a different place.

    b. Going to a *Kiddush* in the middle of the meal, and then returning home and *bentching*.

    c. When you want to go for dessert to someone else's house or to a "*tisch*."

13. **LEFT WITHOUT BENTCHING:** If you forgot or didn't know that you cannot leave, and you left, you should try and go back for *bentching* and על המחיה (not בורא נפשות). If it's difficult to go back and you have some bread with you, you should eat some bread (doesn't have to be a כזית (מ'ב קפד' ס'ק ט') and then *bentch*. (If you were finished eating when you left, you will need to wash again and make a new המוציא.) Even if you don't have any bread to eat there, you can still *bentch* where you are without eating more. (שם סעי' א')

14. The previous עצה is an עצה only if you left without *bentching*, but לכתחלה, of course, you should not leave. If your friend comes over in middle of your סעודה to invite you for dessert, you should first

36

bentch and then go, since you didn't have it in mind by המוציא. (קעח' מ"ב ס"ק לג')

15. **רצה ויעלה ויבוא:** On שבת, יו"ט, ראש חודש, and חול המועד, one has to add or שבת. (רפח' סעי' ה') Even if your סעודה extends well past שבת or רצה or יעלה ויבוא, you still need to add it in since you started your סעודה while it was שבת or יו"ט, etc. The הלכה is that we go after the התחלת סעודה. (שם) If you already *davened* מעריב of חול (מ"ב שם ס"ק לד') or if you said ברוך (סעי' י) המבדיל בין קודש לחול, you do not add in anything anymore. (ע"י מ"ב ס"י רסג' ס"ק סז' שמסופק בזה אם יכול לומר רצה. והגר"ז קפח', יז' והקצות השלחן ס"י מ' סעי' יז' פסקו שלא להזכיר, וכן הביא בוזאת הברכה בשם ר' אלישיב פרק טו' דף 144 אות ג'. וכן בערוך השלחן ס"י קפח' סעי' כג' פסק שלא להזכיר (ואע"פ שבס"י רסג' סעי' כו' כ' שצ"ע אם יכול וכמו המ"ב, מ"מ מבואר שכיון שהוא ספק, שב ואל תעשה עדיף וכמו שכ' האחרונים כן

16. If you started your סעודה on a weekday and it extended into חנוכה, ודאי לילה or פורים, or ראש חודש and you ate a כזית of bread <u>after</u> it was (ד' – page 145 וזאת הברכה), you will need to say יעלה ויבוא or על הניסים. If you ate a כזית of bread only during בין השמשות, you do not add anything. (ודאי לילה is considered שקיעה after 40-45 minutes Approximately) (סי' קפח' מ"ב ס"ק לג')

17. If you started a meal on ראש חודש and it extended into the night which is not ראש חודש, you still say יעלה ויבוא because you go according to when you started your meal. If you *davened* מעריב before *bentching*, you leave out יעלה ויבוא since you already started the next day which is not ראש חודש. (סימן תכד' במשנה ברורה ס"ק ב')

18. If your שלש סעודות (The reason the 3rd meal is called שלש סעודות is because with the last meal you are מקיים all the 3 סעודות – The first 2 you're hungry and it is not proof you're eating לשם שמים, but by the 3rd סעודה that is eaten even when you're not so hungry, that proves that you are eating your סעודות on שבת all לשם שמים – טעמי המנהגים שצז'.) on שבת extends into ראש חודש and you ate a כזית after ודאי לילה, some say to say only יעלה ויבוא and some say to say both רצה and יעלה ויבוא. One can do either one. (מ"ב ס"י קפח' ס"ק לג') One should preferably stay out of this שאלה and avoid eating a כזית of bread after 40 minutes after שקיעה. If שלש סעודות extends into פורים or חנוכה, you only say (קיצור שלחן ערוך מד', יז') רצה. (Since saying על הניסים is a רשות unlike יעלה ויבוא.) (שם במ"ב)

19. **FORGOT יעלה ויבוא or רצה:** If you forget to say רצה or יעלה ויבוא in *bentching*, the following are the הלכות:
   a. As long as you didn't say ה' in בונה ברחמיו ירושלים, stop and go back and say it.

b. If you said 'ה, you can still fix it by saying למדני חוקיך, and then go back and say רצה ויעלה ויבוא. (מ'ב ס'ק כב')

c. If you finished the ברכה but you didn't start the 4ᵗʰ ברכה yet, you can say the special נוסח at that point which is printed in many *Siddurim*. (קפ'ח סעי' ו')

d. If you already started the word ברוך (ביאור הלכה ד'ה עד שהתחיל) of the 4ᵗʰ ברכה, you no longer have a way to fix it up and now the remaining question is whether you have to *bentch* again. The following are the הלכות:

    1. If it is שבת and it is one of the first two סעודות, you must repeat the entire *bentching*. Even if you have a ספק if you said it, you must repeat it. (מ'ב ס'ק טז)

    2. If it's at שלש סעודות, you don't have to *bentch* again since you aren't מחויב to wash. (שם סעי' ח')

    3. If it is י'ט, a man must repeat *bentching*, but for a woman there is a מחלוקת if she must repeat *bentching*, and it would be best either to hear *bentching* from someone else or to eat another כזית of bread and then *bentch* again. (הליכות בת ישראל פ'ג הערה לב')

    4. If it is יום כיפור, ראש השנה, חול המועד, ראש חודש (מ'ב ס'ק יט'), and you forgot יעלה ויבוא, you do not have to repeat *bentching* since there is no חיוב to eat a סעודה on these days. Even if it is also שבת, you do not have repeat *bentching* since the יעלה ויבוא is not because of שבת. (קפ'ח סעי' ז')

20. If you forget to say על הניסים, as long as you didn't say 'ה, you can still say it. If you said 'ה, you can say the הרחמן at the end of *bentching*, but if you didn't, you do not have to repeat *bentching*. (תרפ'ב סעי' א')

21. **ברכה מעין ג':** When eating a שיעור of any מזונות made from the ה' מינים, fruits only from the ז' מינים, or when drinking wine or grape juice, you have to make a ברכה אחת מעין ג', which is either על המחיה, על העץ, or על הגפן. (ס'י רח מ'ב ס'ק נ') If you ate a שיעור of all three, you make one ברכה with all three included; the order is על המחיה first, then על העץ, and then הגפן. (שם סעי' יב')

38

22. If you needed על המחיה and על העץ and you skipped one of them at the end of the ברכה, you should make it again and say the one that you skipped. (וזאת הברכה page 47 – 'ג)

23. If you ate only מזונות, you can only say על המחיה and you <u>cannot</u> add in על העץ. Even if you also ate a few <u>cut-up</u> grapes or <u>cut-up</u> dates, but it was less than a שיעור, you cannot add in על העץ to your על המחיה. (וזאת הברכה page 48 – 'ה; The מחבר says in 'רח' סעי' יח that for any ספק you should not add in to the ברכה אחרונה, and the 'מ'ב ס'ק פב brings the ר'ט that argues, but only by ספק. If you know you don't have a שיעור then you may not add it in.)

24. If you are unsure if you ate a שיעור of the grapes or if you drank a שיעור of יין (מ'ב שם ס'ק פב'), or even if you ate one whole grape or date (which is a בריה and a ספק if you need a ברכה אחרונה – see #27) then you <u>are</u> allowed to add it in if you are making the ברכה מעין ג' anyway on something else. (שם בוזאת הברכה)

25. If you are making על המחיה and בורא נפשות, you are supposed to say על המחיה first since it is more חשוב. (ביאור הלכה רב', יא' ד'ה ברכה) you are בדיעבד יוצא, even if you said it in the wrong order.

26. If you ate פירות חוץ לארץ of the ז' מינים, you say at the end of the ברכה the words ועל הפירות. If you ate פירות ארץ ישראל then you say ועל פירותיה, even if you ate it out of ארץ ישראל. If you drink wine that was produced from grapes grown in ארץ ישראל, you say ועל גפנה. (רח' סעי' י')

27. **EATING A בריה:** A בריה is a whole, complete food. One should avoid eating a בריה in one shot if all that will be eaten is less than a שיעור. The reason is: If you eat a whole fruit, then even if it's less than a שיעור, there are opinions that hold you would have to make a ברכה אחרונה on it since it is חשוב, but since others hold that you do not make a ברכה אחרונה, you will cause yourself a ספק and that should be avoided. Some examples of a בריה are a pomegranate seed, almond, grape, chickpea, bean, cashew, popcorn, sesame seed, sunflower seed (removing the shell doesn't make it not whole), whole fish (sardine), or any natural whole thing. If you eat one almond, you will have a ספק if you need to

make a בורא נפשות and therefore it should be avoided. Eat a lot and then you are good to go. (ס'י ה'י סע'י א')

28. In the following scenarios you avoid this issue:

   a. If you bite it and eat half at a time, that is not considered eating a בריה (שה'יצ אות כא')

   b. If a tiny bit is missing, it is not considered a בריה. Even if you take out the pit, it is not considered whole anymore. If you only eat the flesh of the pomegranate seed and you spit out the seed, it is not included in this ספק. Eating an olive but not its pit is not a בריה. (רמ'א שם ומ'ב ס'ק ז')

   c. If you are in middle of a meal (when you ate the בריה) and you will be *bentching* anyway, or if you ate something else that needs the same ברכה אחרונה as the בריה, then you are covered and you can eat that one grape, almond, bean, or anything else.

   d. Question (tricky): If you ate one chickpea, which, מספק, needs a בורא נפשות, and then you decided to wash on bread, will *bentching* cover the chickpea? Answer: No. Since you ate the chickpea before you started your meal, the chickpea is not part of your meal and *bentching* will not cover it. So, avoid eating just one chickpea before washing. Eat it after washing.

הלכות קדימה בברכות
(ברכות Order of)

CHAPTER VI

הלכות ברכות

CHAPTER VI – הלכות ברכות
הלכות קדימה בברכות

1. **קדימה בברכות:** When eating different foods, whether they have the same ברכה or different ברכות, there is a specific order how to eat them. If the ברכות are the same, then the food that is more חשוב will take precedence, and if the ברכות are different, then the ברכה that is more חשוב will take precedence. In this section, we will explain how to determine what makes a ברכה or food more חשוב than another, but before doing so, there are a few facts you must know.

2. The orders of preference that we will learn are the לכתחלה way to make ברכות, but בדיעבד, if you did not follow the right order, you are still יוצא and you do not make the ברכות again in the right order. (רמ'א ס' (ריא' סעי' ה'

3. The application of which ברכה goes first is only relevant when both foods are in front of you and you want to eat both foods. If, however, you do not want both foods, or even if you do but the other food is in a different room, you do not have to go get the other food and you can eat the food in front of you first. (רמ'א שם ומ'ב ס'ק א')

4. If the custom is to eat in a certain order, then these הלכות do not apply. For example, if you normally start off your meal with soup or a fruit cup and then the main course follows, you may eat the soup first, which might be a שהכל or האדמה, and then the main course even if it is a מזונות. (כף החיים ריא' א')

5. If you have an explicit reason to go out of order, you can. We all make a קידוש on הגפן before washing, even though המוציא usually comes first. The reason it is okay is because we cannot eat before קידוש. The same is true if you are very thirsty and you must drink something before eating; you may do so even if you plan on eating something immediately afterwards, such as a מזונות, which would normally come before a שהכל. (וזאת הברכה page 127 'א-')

6. There are four scenarios, each with their own הלכות:
    a. **Two or more foods with different ברכות.**
    b. **Two or more foods with the same ברכה.**
    c. **One fruit/food from the ז' מינים and one that is not.**
    d. **Two or more fruits from the ז' מינים.**

7. **TWO OR MORE FOODS WITH <u>DIFFERENT</u> ברכות:**
When you want to eat different foods that have different ברכות, you must figure out which ברכה goes first because you are מחויב to make the **<u>ברכה</u>** that is more חשוב first.

8. The order of חשיבות for all ברכות are: (שם מ'ב ס'ק לה')
   a. **המוציא**
   b. **מזונות**
   c. **הגפן**
   d. **העץ**
   e. **האדמה**
   f. **שהכל**
   g. **ריח**

9. The reason for this order is: The ברכה that is more specific is more חשוב. A המוציא is the most specific ברכה in that it refers only to bread. A שהכל is the least specific as it refers to everything. (הגפן is more specific than מזונות but מזונות is more חשוב since it gives more sustenance.)

10. Examples:
    a. Soda, pretzels, and a peach – You make a מזונות, then a העץ, and lastly a שהכל.

    b. Banana, dates, and grape juice – You make a הגפן first, then a העץ, and lastly a האדמה.

    c. Soft pretzel, La-Hit bar, fruit roll-up – You make a מזונות and then a שהכל.

    d. בשמים, orange juice, spelt cookies, and almonds – You make a מזונות first, then a העץ, then a שהכל, and lastly a בשמים בורא מיני.

11. The list in #8 is the order of חשיבות and remains true even if something later on the list is more חביב, is from the ז' מינים, or is שלם/whole (מ'ב ס'ק לה'):
    a. Spelt cake or rice cakes and olives – The מזונות on the cake is first even though olives are from the ז' מינים.

b. Apple and chocolate – The העץ on the apple is first even though the chocolate is more חביב to you.

c. Piece of a cookie and a whole banana – The מזונות on the cookie is first even though the banana is a שלם.

12. **TWO OR MORE FOODS WITH THE <u>SAME</u> ברכה:**
When eating two foods that have the same ברכה, you have to make the ברכה on the food that is more חשוב. The following list is how to determine which food is more חשוב (מ'ב ס'ק לה'):
   a. **ז' מינים - Fruits from the שבעת המינים**
   b. **שלם - Whole**
   c. **חביב - Preferred (you like it better)**
   d. **גדול – Big**

13. Examples:
   a. Half a cookie (white flour) and whole pieces of rice – You make the מזונות on the cookie even though it is not שלם since the ז' מינים is more חשוב than שלם.

   b. Grapes and an apple – You make the העץ on the grape since it is from the ז' מינים even if the grape is cut up and even if you like apples better.

   c. Sliced pastrami and sliced corned beef – You make the שהכל on the one you like better. (Since they are both not from the ז' מינים and they are both not שלם.)

   d. Whole bar of chocolate and a lollypop – You make the שהכל on the one you like better. (They are both not from the ז' מינים and are both whole.)

   e. Whole chocolate-chip cookies and some pieces of those cookies – You make the מזונות on a whole cookie since it is שלם and more חשוב.

   f. Whole cinnamon rugelach and cut-up black-and-white cookies – You make the מזונות on the whole rugelach even if you like the black-and-white cookies better since שלם precedes חביב.

14. **מזונות:**

Following are some הלכות pertaining to the ברכה of מזונות:

   a. **ה' מינים**

   b. **Rice**

   c. **פת הבא בכיסנין**

15. **ה' מינים:** The second most חשוב is the ברכה of מזונות, which includes anything made from the ה' מינים. If you have a choice of different types of מזונות that are made from different grains, the order of חשיבות is the following (קסח' סעי' ד' ומ"ב ס"ק יג'):

   a. **חטה - Wheat**

   b. **שעורה - Barley**

   c. **כוסמין - Spelt**

   d. **שיפון - Rye**

   e. **שבולת שועל – Oats**

16. The above order remains true even if a grain that is later on the list is more חביב to you. (מ"ב שם ובסי' ריא' ס"ק כ'):

   a. Chocolate-chip cookies made of wheat and cookies made of spelt – You make the ברכה on the wheat cookies even if you like spelt better.

   b. White wheat bread and rye bread – You make the ברכה on white bread even if you like rye bread better.

   c. Crackers from white flour and a bowl of barley – You make the ברכה on the crackers, even if the barley is more חביב to you.

17. **RICE:** Rice is a מזונות but not from the ה' מינים; therefore, it is less חשוב than other foods that are מזונות. If you want to eat rice and some crackers, you should make your מזונות on the crackers and not on the rice. (Have in mind the rice.) However, rice is more חשוב than העץ, האדמה, ושהכל.

(What remains unclear is whether rice precedes הגפן or not. Do we say that since it is a מזונות it is earlier on the list and it comes first, or since a הגפן has two מעלות, in that it's a more specific ברכה and also that it is from the ה' מינים, maybe it should be considered more חשוב than rice?) (In וזאת הברכה page 125 אות ג', he says that it comes before הגפן, but in Rabbi Forst's sefer page 159, it puts a הגפן before rice. In Rabbi Bodner's sefer he brings both שיטות and he is not מכריע.)

18. **פת הבא בכיסנין:** When it comes to a מזונות food, some foods have similarities to actual bread and some don't. Any food that is מזונות and is similar to bread is called פת הבא בכיסנין. A מזונות that is פת הבא בכיסנין takes precedence over non-פת הבא בכיסנין. Since the הלכה on פת הבא is that you have to wash if you were to be קובע סעודה on פת הבא בכיסנין, it is considered more חשוב. (גר"ז סדר ברכת הנהנין פ'ט אות ו', ז') (What still needs עיון is: What takes precedence, חביב or שלם or פת הבא בכיסנין)

19. Example: If you have macaroni-and-cheese and crackers, you should make your מזונות on the cracker since it is פת הבא בכיסנין, and macaroni is not. (A question that still remains: What if you like the macaroni better or if the macaroni is whole and the crackers are not?)

20. **חביב:** See #13c,d where the הלכה is to make the ברכה on the one that is more חביב to you. The following is the definition of חביב: (מחבר ריא' סעי' א') (ומ'ב ס'ק י' ובסוף ס'ק לה')

    a. What you normally like better, even if right now you prefer to eat the other one first, is considered חביב.

    b. If in your choices of foods there isn't one that you normally prefer, then the one you prefer right now is considered the one that is more חביב.

21. Once you take a small bite of the one that is more חביב you can then eat the other one first. (שם במ'ב ס'ק י')

22. **ONE FRUIT/FOOD FROM THE ז' מינים AND ONE THAT IS NOT:** Fruits from the ז' מינים are more חשוב than other fruits. Therefore, if you are eating a fruit from the ז' מינים and a fruit/food that is not from the ז' מינים, you make העץ on the ז' מינים fruit, even if you like the other one better. (סי' ריא' סעי' א')

23. EXAMPLES:

    a. A grape and apple: The ברכה is made on the grape.

    b. A date and cashew: The ברכה is made on the date.

    c. Pomegranate seeds and a peach: The ברכה is made on the seeds. (All the above is true even if you like the other fruit better)

24. **TWO OR MORE FRUITS FROM THE ז' מינים:**

If you are eating two or more fruits from the ז' מינים, the determination on which fruit to make the ברכה is based on the order of the פסוק. The fruits closer to the word ארץ are more חשוב. The פסוק says ארץ חטה ושעורה גפן תאנה ורמון, ארץ זית שמן ודבש. Grapes, figs, and pomegranates are 3, 4, 5, after the word ארץ, and olives and honey/dates are 1, 2 after the word ארץ. Therefore, the proper order is: (סי' ריא' סעי' ד')

   a. Olives
   b. Dates
   c. Grapes
   d. Figs
   e. Pomegranates

25. This order holds true even if you like the less חשוב one better and even if it is whole and the other is not. (מחבר שם סעי' א' מ'ב ס'ק לה')

26. **EXAMPLES:**

   a. If you are eating grapes and dates, you make the ברכה on the date since it is first in the פסוק. This is true even if you like grapes better.

   b. If you are eating a whole fig and cut-up olives, you make the ברכה on the olives since it is more חשוב even though the figs are whole and the olives are not.

   c. If you are eating grapes and drinking wine, the wine goes first because wine is more חשוב. (רמ'א שם סעי' ד')

27. **FOOD AND DRINK:**

If you have a food and a drink that are both שהכל, the **food** does __not__ automatically take precedence; rather, whatever is שלם or חביב decides. (מ'ב לה) (This is the משמעות to me from the המ'ב סתימת and so says the וזאת הברכה page 125- ז' but in the ערוך ריא' סעיף יז') he says that a מאכל always comes first.) השלחן

28. **EXCEPTION:**

On the list of preference when eating foods that have different ברכות, a העץ comes before האדמה. However, this is only true if the two

foods are **<u>exactly</u>** equal. If they are not equal, then the one that is
more חשוב comes first. This translates as: If the האדמה is more חביב
or from the ז' מינים (for example: whole wheat kernels), or it is a שלם and
the עץ is not, then the האדמה goes first. The reason is that since the
two ברכות are very close in חשיבות, the עץ only takes precedence if
they are exactly equal. (מ'ב ריא' ס'ק לה')

29. To figure out the order for the previous הלכה, the following is the
    order:
    a. חביב
    b. ז' מינים
    c. שלם (in the שער הציון ס'ק ה' he has a ספק if שלם is first or last, so one should try and stay out of this שאלה.)

30. **EXAMPLES:**
    a. If you are eating grapes and a banana and you like bananas
       better, you make a האדמה on the banana before the עץ on the
       grape. ז' מינים precedes חביב.

    b. If you are eating a whole cucumber and cut-up apples, which
       are both not from the ז' מינים, and you like them the same, you
       make האדמה first since the cucumber is whole.

31. **EXPLANATION:** Why is this order in #29 different than the order in
    #12? Here in #29, חביב comes first and there in #12, ז' מינים comes
    first. The reason is: Where the ברכות are the same, the criterion
    deciding which comes first is which food is more חשוב, and ז' מינים
    food is intrinsically more חשוב than what is חביב to you personally.
    However, when deciding between עץ and האדמה, we decide by
    seeing which ברכה is more חשוב, and since the purpose of a ברכה is
    to give שבח to ה', when making a ברכה on something that is more
    חביב, you naturally give more שבח, which makes that ברכה more
    חשוב. (וזאת הברכה בבירור הלכה נב')

32. EXAMPLES BASED ON ALL OF THE ABOVE:

a. Chicken and corn – and you like chicken better: You make a האדמה first, which is more חשוב even though the chicken is more חביב.

b. An apple and a melon – and you like melon better: You make a האדמה first since you like melons better and by העץ and האדמה what is חביב goes first.

c. A peach and a wheat rice cake (which is a האדמה) – and you like both the same: You make a האדמה first since it is from the ז' מינים.

d. A peach and wheat rice cake – and you like the peach better: You make a העץ since it is more חביב to you, which precedes the ז' מינים when it's a choice between העץ and האדמה.

e. A date, wine, and a cookie: You make a העץ ← הגפן ← מזונות.

f. Farina from wheat and cooked barley: You make a מזונות on the farina since wheat comes before שעורים on the list of the ה' מינים.

g. A whole portabella mushroom and a piece of chicken: You make a שהכל on the whole mushroom because a שלם comes before a piece.

h. Whole peas and cut-up carrots – and you like carrots better: You make a האדמה on the peas first since שלם precedes חביב.

i. Cooked rice and potatoes: You make a מזונות first because even a מזונות of rice comes before האדמה.

j. Whole cookies and pieces of cookies or cake – and you like them all the same: You make the מזונות on the whole cookie.

k. An olive, a date, and pineapple – and you like the date best, then the pineapple, and then the olive: You make a האדמה on the pineapple first and then a העץ on the olive. (The reason: First you put together all the fruits of העץ and the olive wins, as it is first of מינים ז'; then between an olive and pineapple, since you like the pineapple better, it wins. וזאת הברכה page 126 - #12.)

33. As we learned in #8, the proper order of ברכות is the לכתחלה way to make ברכות, but בדיעבד if you did not follow the הלכה, you will not have to repeat anything:

   a. If you made a שהכל before a מזונות, all you do is now make a מזונות and you do not have to say a שהכל again.

   b. If you made a מזונות on rice before a wheat cracker, you do not have to make another מזונות and you can just eat the cracker, even if the cracker is more חשוב than the rice, as long as you had the cracker in mind when you made your מזונות.

החליף ברכה בחברתה
(Made the wrong ברכה)

CHAPTER VII

הלכות ברכות

החליף ברכה בחברתה

1. **MADE THE WRONG ברכה:** Even though לכתחלה one is always supposed to make the proper ברכה, there are instances where the "wrong" ברכה will suffice בדיעבד. There are ברכות that are specific and there are ברכות that are more general. If the ברכה you made incorporates the food you made your ברכה on, then בדיעבד it will be sufficient.

2. **IMPORTANT:** Following, there are many instances that you are יוצא with the "wrong" ברכה and you are allowed to continue eating without making a new ברכה. Not only may you continue eating without a ברכה, but the הלכה is, you may not make a new ברכה since the rule is, ספק ברכות לקולא. In cases where you are יוצא and there is no מחלוקת, then you may just continue eating. However, if there is a מחלוקת if you are יוצא, then, if possible, one should try and make a ברכה on another food that will get you the ברכה you need, or to try and hear someone else making the ברכה you would need. (מ"ב ס"י קס"ד ס"ק מט') If these two עצות are not possible, then you may just continue eating.

3. **שהכל:**

   A שהכל could apply to every food, as you are saying that ה' created everything. It is the most general ברכה and the meaning of the ברכה is true about every food, so even though one should only make a שהכל on the proper foods, if you made a שהכל on any food you are יוצא, and you may just continue eating. (סי' ה' סע' א')

4. If one who learned all of הלכות ברכות has a ספק about what ברכה to make on a specific food, he or she has a right to make a שהכל on that food. If one is missing information that can be determined, then one cannot make a שהכל since it is possible to solve the ספק. One who did not learn all of הלכות ברכות cannot just make a שהכל when unsure what ברכה a particular food requires. (רמ"א ס' רב' מ"ב ס"ק פד')

5. **המוציא:**

   A המוציא can only be made on לחם/bread. פת הבא בכיסנין has certain aspects of לחם and therefore בדיעבד if you make a המוציא instead of a מזונות you are יוצא. (כף החיים קס"ח מג') If you make a המוציא on other foods that are מזונות but not פת הבא בכיסנין, like farina or pasta or very thin and flat pancakes, you are not יוצא and you would need to make a מזונות. A המוציא on anything else is no good and you must make a new ברכה.

6. הגפן:

A הגפן is only made on יין/wine/grape juice. However, if you made a הגפן on a grape or a raisin, בדיעבד it is good, since the ברכה you said is true, because a grape/raisin does indeed grow on a vine. (ס"י רח' סע' טו') A הגפן on anything else is invalid and you must make a new ברכה.

7. מזונות:

A מזונות is said on anything that is made from the ה' מינים and rice. If you made a מזונות on any other food, except water or salt, it is a מחלוקת if you are יוצא. The word מזונות means that the food nourishes the body. Some hold that since all foods nourish, בדיעבד a מזונות is a good ברכה on all foods except water and salt, which don't nourish. (ביאור הלכה קס"ז סע" י' ד"ה במקום) Others disagree and say that other foods do not nourish the same way that regular מזונות foods do, and it is therefore not a good ברכה even בדיעבד. In this situation, since the rule is ספק ברכות להקל, you cannot just make a new ברכה, because you might have been יוצא already. One should either make a new ברכה on something else that wasn't included in the ברכה or find someone else making a מזונות to be מוציא you. If these two עצות are not feasible, then you may just continue eating, because ספק ברכות לקולא. (סימן קס"ז סע' ט' ום'ב ס"ק מט') (According to Rav Moshe Feinstein ('או'ח ד', סימן מ)): In this case, if you mistakenly made a מזונות and didn't start eating yet, or if you only ate less than a כזית, then there is a הידור to make a שינוי מקום and then make a new ברכה. If you already ate a כזית in which case a שינוי מקום won't help, then you can just continue eating if you can't employ the other עצות (since it is only a הידור). (Rav Moshe only gives this עצה by מזונות where it is a מחלוקת. The same applies to העץ on wine, and to a האדמה on bread or any מזונות food, where there is a מחלוקת if you are יוצא, but to all other cases where everyone agrees that you are יוצא then you may just continue eating.)

8. Some examples:

   a. If you made a שהכל on a cookie, you may continue eating and no new ברכה is necessary.

   b. If you made a הגפן on a grape, you may continue eating and no new ברכה is necessary.

   c. If you made a הגפן on orange juice, you are not יוצא. Stop drinking and make a שהכל right away.

d. If you made a מזונות on potato chips, try and make a האדמה on some other food, or be יוצא from someone else making a האדמה, but if these עצות are not available, you may just continue eating.

9. העץ:

A העץ should only be made on fruit that grow on trees that produce fruits from year to year. If you made a העץ on wine, it is a מחלוקת if you are יוצא, and since the rule is ספק ברכות להקל you cannot just make a new ברכה, meaning a הגפן. (סי' רח' מ'ב ס'ק ע') Try and listen to a הגפן from someone else, but if not, you may continue drinking.

10. If one made a העץ on a fruit peel or raw sour cherry or pureed fruit, which are all שהכל, it is valid בדיעבד since they are all essentially fruits of a tree, and you may just continue eating. (סי' רח' מ'ב ס'ק ג' - רמ'א סי' רב' סעי' ז')

11. **BERRIES:** Certain berries, depending on how they grow, will require a האדמה or a העץ. בדיעבד one who recites a העץ on the berries that are really a האדמה can continue eating. The same is true if you made a העץ on a banana, strawberry, or pineapple, since they essentially grow on a tree. (In the case of a strawberry, the מ'ב says to eat only a little bit so as not to make it a ברכה לבטלה, and then stop, since only a few יחידים hold that it is a העץ) (סי' רג' ס'ק ג)

12. האדמה:

A האדמה should be made on all foods that grow directly from the ground. If you made a האדמה on fruits, בדיעבד you are יוצא, and you may continue eating without a new ברכה since it is also true that fruits grow out from the ground. The same is **not** true if you made a העץ on a food that is האדמה as it is <u>not</u> true that a carrot grows on a tree. (סי' רח' סעי' א')

13. If one made a האדמה on bread or on a food that is מזונות, there is a מחלוקת if it is valid בדיעבד, so one may not just make a new ברכה. (The מחלוקת is whether you say that bread and מזונות come from the earth and it is valid, or since it is no longer a פרי then a פרי האדמה is wrong) You should try and make the ברכה you need on another food or to hear it from someone else. If they are not options, you may just continue eating.

14. ברכות האחרונות:

One should always make the appropriate ברכה אחרונה. However, there are times that even if the "wrong" ברכה אחרונה was made,

בדיעבד it will be sufficient, and there are times that it will not be sufficient.

15. **If you need to say ברכת המזון and instead you made a:**

    a. **בורא נפשות:** you are not יוצא. (עי' סי' רח' מ'ב ס'ק סב' – ולכאורה כן הוא באופן זה)

    b. **על העץ/על הגפן:** you are not יוצא. (פשוט)

    c. **על המחיה**

        1. It is a מחלוקת if you are יוצא, and therefore, if possible, you should wash again with על נטילת ידים (if you left the table and you were מסיח דעת from eating), make a new המוציא and eat another כביצה of bread, and then *bentch*. (א'- page 209 - וזאת הברכה בשם ר' אלישב) Or, if someone else is *bentching*, he can be מוציא you.

        2. If the previous עצות are not feasible, then if you ate כדי שביעה — an amount of food that filled you up to satisfaction — then you should *bentch*. (ר' שלמה פרנקל שליט'א – עי' סי' רט' (סעי' ג' ומ'ב ס'ק י')

        3. The previous הלכה is only true if you made the על המחיה and later you realized what you did, but if you started off saying על המחיה and in middle of the ברכה or right after you finished you realized that you were supposed to *bentch*, you can continue with נודה לך since you are יוצא the first ברכה of *bentching* with על המחיה. (עי' סי' קפז' סעיף א' ובמ'ב ס'ק ד')

16. **If you need to make על המחיה and instead you made:**

    a. **בורא נפשות:** you are not יוצא. (סי' רב' מ'ב ס'ק מב')

    b. **על העץ/הגפן:** you are not יוצא. (ד- page 209 וזאת הברכה)

    c. **ברכת המזון:** you <u>are</u> יוצא. (סי' רח' מ'ב ס'ק עה')

        1. *Bentching* will also cover rice even though it needs a בורא נפשות, the reason being that it is a satisfying food. (שם)

        2. The same applies to wine or dates; if you ate a שיעור and you need על העץ/הגפן, you will be יוצא with *bentching* since these two also give a lot of satisfaction. (שם)

        3. If you started *bentching* on מזונות, rice, יין ותמרים, if you realize your mistake after the first ברכה then you just stop, and you are יוצא with just the first ברכה. (מחבר סי' רח' סעי' יז')

        4. If you started *bentching* instead of על המחיה, and you remembered before finishing the first ברכה, you should

stop at that point (the beginning of the ברכה is paramount to the first part of the ברכה of מעין שלש) and then continue with the words from נודה לך and then continue with ועל שהנחלת לאבותינו ארץ חמדה וטובה ורחבה (which is from the second part of the מעין שלש) and then continue with רחם נא in על in רחם נא (שם) (This way you said all three parts of המחיה על המחיה).

17. If you need to make על הגפן and instead you made:

a. **ברכת המזון:** you are יוצא. (סי' רח' סעי' יז')

b. **על העץ:** you are יוצא. (ביאור הלכה סוף סי' רח ד'ה מספק)

c. **על המחיה:** you are יוצא. (כף החיים סי' רח' אות פט')

d. **בורא נפשות:** you are not יוצא. (סי' רח' סעי' יג' ועי' סי' רב' מ'ב ס'ק מב')

(The reason you are יוצא with the first three is because wine (and dates) satiates more so than other foods, and therefore *bentching* and על המחיה apply. An על העץ is also good since wine comes from grapes.)

18. If you need to make על העץ and instead you made:

a. **ברכת המזון:** you are not יוצא, besides dates. (סי' רח' סעי' יד' ועי' מ'ב ס'ק עה' דדוקא (על מיני מזונות יוצא בדיעבד)

b. **על המחיה:** you are not יוצא. (כף החיים סי' רח אות פט')

c. **על הגפן:** you are not יוצא unless it is grapes. (סי' רח סעי' טו')

d. **בורא נפשות:** you are not יוצא. (סי' רח' סעי' יג' ועי' סי' רב' מ'ב ס'ק מב')

19. If you need to make בורא נפשות and instead you made:

a. **ברכת המזון:** you are not יוצא. (סי' רח' סעי' יד' ועי' מ'ב ס'ק עה' דדוקא על מיני מזונות יוצא בדיעבד)

b. **על המחיה:** you are not יוצא. (Except for rice) (למוד מברכת המזון)

c. **מעין שלש:** you are not יוצא, unless it is fruit – then על העץ will suffice בדיעבד. (סי' רח' סעי' יג' ומ'ב ס'ק סב')

20. Miscellaneous הלכות for ברכה אחרונה:

a. If you eat both fruits that are from the ז' מינים and fruits that are not from the ז' מינים then all you make is על העץ. (רח' סעי' יג')

b. If you eat both cake and rice, all you make is על המחיה. (כף החיים רח' מא')

c. If you ate a meal but didn't wash and had foods that would require בורא נפשות, על העץ, על המחיה, and a בורא נפשות, and instead of making all three you *bentched*, the *bentching* suffices for the foods needing על המחיה but you still need to make על העץ and a בורא נפשות. (אות ו' page 210 וזאת הברכה)

פת הבא בכיסנין

CHAPTER VIII

הלכות ברכות

1. When you eat לחם/פת/bread, you make a המוציא/בהמ'ז. (קסח סע' ט) The reason bread has its own special ברכה is: It is the main food source and there is no other food that satiates like it. Until modern times, a meal always consisted of bread and a secondary item to go along with it. Even though nowadays people do not like to wash, bread still retains its status.

2. **What is halachic פת?**
   a. It is made from the ה' מינים.
   b. It is normally eaten as a main part of a meal.
   c. It is baked and not cooked. (שיש ,עי' סימן קסח' סע' יג' בבלילה עבה שאין בה מי פירות שבישלה

   מחלוקת אם אבד תוריתא דנהמא. וירא שמים יאכל תוך הסעודה. ויש נפקא מינה בסופגנים שמטוגנים בשמן עמוק ואחר הטיגון
   (מוסיף "קוסטורד" או שוקולוד

3. "Bread" made from other grains is not המוציא. For example, corn or bean bread that is made purely from corn or bean flour is a שהכל. Rice bread is a מזונות. If wheat flour is mixed in, then depending on how much is added it might be המוציא. (עי' סי' רח' סע' ח' – ט)

4. Even real bread that was subsequently cooked or deep-fried (בישול בשמן עמוק
   חשיבא בישול - וזאת הברכה פרק ג' דף 23 אות ג' בשם הגר'ז, שש'כ, ר' אלישב) at times loses its status of bread. For example, if you cut up real bread into pieces smaller than a כזית and then deep-fry them for croutons, they become a מזונות since they lose their bread status. (סי' קסח' סע' י)

5. **What is פת הבא בכיסנין?**
   Many products are made from the ה' מינים and are baked, but they are not eaten as the mainstay of a meal, rather only as a snack. These products that are eaten as snacks are called פת הבא בכיסנין, which literally means "bread with a pocket." The ברכה you make on פה'ב is a מזונות and על המחיה (קסח סע' ו' מ'ב ס'ק כג). (As will be explained, if you are קובע סעודה on these products, you will need to wash and *bentch*.)

6. Food made from the ה' מינים that is cooked/deep-fried is called a מעשה קדירה, is not considered פת at all, and is always מזונות and על המחיה. Some examples of this are: oatmeal, farina, and couscous. (סי' רח' סע' ב)

7. פת הבא בכיסנין is a product of the ה' מינים that is baked but which most do not eat as a meal-type food, rather only as a snack, and is therefore not a המוציא. One must make a מזונות and על המחיה. (מ'ב קסח' ס'ק כג')

8. **There are 3 types of פת הבא בכיסנין** (ס'י קסח' סעי' ז'):
   a. Regular dough that is baked with a filling of fruit or other sweet things, even if the sweet things are just on top of the dough (**and not just added afterwards**). (This is why these snacks are called bread with a pocket)
   b. Dough that is made from מי פירות/fruit juices.
   c. Dough that is baked till it is dry and cracker-like.

9. In each of these types there is a quality of regular פת that is missing. Regular פת is made from mainly flour and water, has no filling, and is usually soft and somewhat fluffy and has air pockets.

10. Also, in the first two types, the filling or juice must be an amount that significantly changes the taste of the "bread." Adding a few chocolate chips or raisins to a challah does not make it פת הבא בכיסנין. (מ'ב קסח' ס'ק לג')

11. The following chart shows many examples of the different types of פת הבא בכיסנין.

TYPE #1 FILLING	TYPE #2 SWEET DOUGH	TYPE #3 CRACKER LIKE/NOT TOO BRITTLE	TYPE #4 NON-פת הבא בכיסנין
Cheese danish	Pizza		Lasagna/pasta
Cherry danish	Cake		Ravioli
Pizza	Donut	Hard pretzels	Kreplach
Donut (thick dough, deep-fried w/filling)	Franks 'n blanks	Biscuits	Hot cereals
Egg roll (baked)	Egg roll	Cookies	Cooked barley
Potato knish	Cupcakes	Kichel	Bran flakes
Boureka	Knish	Breadsticks	Very thin pancakes
Franks 'n blanks	Cookies	Melba toast	Couscous
Pizza snaps	Boureka	Flatbread	Blintzes
Garlic knots	Pancakes	Crackers	Thin wafers
	Croissants	Pita chips	Donuts (liquid batter - deep fried)
	Soft pretzels		Mandlen (yellow deep-fried)
	Sweet rolls		Matzoh balls
			Egg roll (deep-fried)

12. Regarding all the foods in the first three columns, one normally only makes a מזונות and על המחיה, except in two instances when one will have to wash and *bentch*:

    a.   If it is an item that is generally eaten as a meal. Since most eat it as a meal and not just as a snack, it takes on a דין of real bread. (קסח' סעי' י' מ'ב ס'ק צד')

    b.   If one were to eat an amount that would be a קביעת סעודה. (קסח' סי' ו')

13. Even if the amount of the סעודה is not eaten בכדי אכילת פרס, all the food eaten in your "meal" no matter how long it takes, combines to create the חיוב to wash and *bentch*. (וזאת הברכה פרק ד' דף 27 אות ב')

14. What is the שיעור for a קביעת סעודה? It is a מחלוקת. Some say it is 3–4 ביצים, which is approximately 6–8 כזיתים, and some say it is measured based on the normal amount an average person (of your type) would eat during a meal. (מ'ב קסח' ס'ק כד') Which type of meal? Some say a weekday meal, and some say a שבת meal. (שערי תשובה קסח' סעי' ו' אות ד') There is a big difference between the two. Since it is not clear, one should definitely not eat excessively, which would require *bentching*.

15. The משנה ברורה (שם) says you should stay out of this question and either eat less than 4 ביצים or just wash on bread, because if you eat more than 4 ביצים and less than a full סעודה then you will have a ספק if you need to *bentch*.

16. The following is an example of the שיעור סעודה based on Rabbi Bodner's *shiurim*: If one normally would eat 4 pieces of rye bread (middle slices from a large loaf of standard bakery bread) for a meal, that equals approximately 16 כזיתים. The equivalent to that would be:

    a.   40 sandwich cookies

    b.   12 rugelach

    c.   2 ¾ big black-and-white cookies

    d.   28 small chocolate chip cookies

    e.   3½ average-size muffins.

17. If you ate the amount of the above examples, you would perhaps have to *bentch*. So don't eat that much in one sitting.

18. If when you started to eat you didn't plan on eating a שיעור and you made a מזונות, and then you realized that you will indeed eat a שיעור, then you will need to *bentch*. So, for example, if you wash for two slices of pizza and you planned on eating only one, if you then decide to eat a second one, you will need to *bentch* even though you made a מזונות.

19. If you started out thinking you would have a שיעור and you washed, and then you changed your mind and didn't eat a שיעור, you do not *bentch* and instead you make על המחיה. So, for example, if you washed for two slices and then only ate one, you will make על המחיה. (Some wash and *bentch* even on only a כזית of pizza, which, according to Rabbi Bodner, is one-ninth of a slice!)

20. Rav Moshe says that a שיעור סעודה is based upon the average person in his or her particular type. Men are one group, women another, children yet another, and older and younger people all create their own groups. If women generally only eat one slice of pizza for a meal, then that would be a שיעור סעודה for them and would require washing. (אג'מ אוח'ג לב')

21. **EXAMPLES:**

    a. **PIZZA:** Some say that for pizza one has to wash for even one bite since it is generally eaten as a meal. Some say it is considered a snack food and therefore you need to eat an amount that is קביעות סעודה, which some say is two slices. Some say that women, who usually only eat one slice, have to wash on one slice. Ask your *rav*.

    b. **CALZONES:** Big calzones that are usually eaten as a meal require a המוציא.

    c. **PIZZA SNAPS:** Small pizza snaps are made for a snack and not eaten as a meal, so they are מזונות. If one eats a very large amount, then it would require המוציא and *bentching*.

d. **MELBA TOAST:** These have the third quality of פת הבא בכיסנין and are made to eat as a snack and therefore are מזונות. (If you eat a very large amount you will need to wash and bentch.)

e. **SWEET ROLLS:** These are eaten as a snack since they are too sweet to eat like bread and are מזונות. If one eats a large amount, it will require המוציא and *bentching*.

f. **BOUREKAS:** These are smaller than calzones and not made for a meal, so they are מזונות.

g. **MATZOH/CRACKERS:** Regular-size matzoh and cracker-size matzoh are made from the same exact ingredients and have different ברכות. The reason: they both have the third quality of פת הבא בכיסנין but the large matzos are made to eat in a meal while the crackers are not.

h. **SOFT PRETZELS:** These can be made in one of two ways. Some are made with just flour and water, and some companies add fruit juices to them. If the added juices make the pretzel significantly sweet (it doesn't taste like bread) then it would be a מזונות since it is made for a snack. If the ingredients are merely flour and water, then one should wash on it. (Some say that it is still a מזונות since it is made for a snack.)

i. **GARLIC KNOTS:** These are either baked or deep-fried. This is bread that is baked/fried, with a garlic paste smeared on top. If the knots are larger than a כזית (usually they are) and the garlic taste is strong, since it is made for a snack, it is a מזונות. If the garlic taste is weak, then it is a המוציא. (Some say that even if it has a weak taste, it is a מזונות since it is made for snack.) If the knots are smaller than a כזית, which is unusual, and they are **deep-fried**, then they would be a מזונות. (See 25.d)

j. **FRENCH TOAST:** This is bread that is fried in a little oil. If you cut the bread into pieces smaller than a כזית and you deep-fry them, they would be a מזונות; otherwise, it is a המוציא. Usually, it is larger than a כזית and not deep-fried, and therefore it's a המוציא.

k. **MEZONOS BREAD:** Many, if not most, hold that it is a המוציא since it tastes like bread and is meant for a meal. Ask your *rav*.

22. The fourth column in the chart above in #11 shows foods that are **not** פת הבא בכיסנין, and no matter how much you eat of those foods you will not make a המוציא and *bentch*. They have no תואר לחם, resemblance of bread, at all and always require a מזונות and על המחיה.

23. The reason they are **not** פת הבא בכיסנין is either:
    a. They are made of very thin dough that didn't rise, and they are very brittle, which doesn't resemble bread. (מ"ב קסח ס"ק לח)
    b. It is dough or grain that is cooked and doesn't have a resemblance of bread. (קסח' סעי' יג ברמ"א)

24. **EXAMPLES OF NON פת הבא בכיסנין:**
    a. **Pasta** – is cooked dough.
    b. **Farina** – is cooked dough.
    c. **Oatmeal** – is cooked grains.
    d. **Blintzes** – are very thin and cooked.
    e. **Thin wafers** – very thin and brittle.

25. **PITA CHIPS AND BREAD CROUTONS:**
    a. If they are made initially with the intention to be a snack, then they are מזונות. (If they are just baked, they **are** considered פת הבא בכיסנין)
    b. If they were first made as bread and then baked further to harden them, they are המוציא.
    c. If they were made as bread and then deep-fried, and the pieces are **larger** than a כזית, they are המוציא. (סימן קסח סעי' י)
    d. If they were made as bread and then deep-fried, and they're **smaller** than a כזית, they are מזונות and על המחיה no matter how much you eat. Since they were cooked, they are **not** considered פת הבא בכיסנין. (שם)
    e. Restaurants often serve bread croutons; you must determine how they are made in order to know if you must wash on them.

26. EATING פת הבא בכיסנין IN A BREAD MEAL:

Usually, one has to make a ברכה on anything that is not a meal-type food and is eaten within a bread meal, because the המוציא doesn't cover it. For example, candy or chocolate eaten within a bread meal still needs a ברכה ראשונה. A snack that is a מזונות and is not פת הבא בכיסנין — for example, Bissli — also needs a ברכה ראשונה. However, one does not make a מזונות on פת הבא בכיסנין within a bread meal, since it has qualities of bread, unless it has all three qualities of פת הבא בכיסנין. Pie is an example of a food that has all three qualities, and if it is being eaten as a dessert (meaning, you are not really hungry anymore), you would have to make a ברכה of מזונות on it. (Rabbi Bodner Addendum Two B.1. and footnote 11)

ה׳ מינים

CHAPTER IX

הלכות ברכות

1. The 5 grains are חטה, שעורה, כוסמין, שיפון, שיבולת שועל – wheat, barley, spelt, rye, and oats. (קסח' סעי' ד מ'ב ס'ק יג)

2. These 5 grains, when eaten whole and raw and they taste good, are a האדמה. If you cook them and they remain separate and not sticky at all, they also remain a האדמה. If they are cooked and stick together or if they are made into flour and added to ingredients, they become a מזונות. Bread made from these 5 grains become a המוציא for which you must wash and *bentch*.

3. All other grains (besides rice), like buckwheat, millet, quinoa, corn, etc., will never become a מזונות or המוציא. If the grains are eaten whole, they are a האדמה and if they are made into flour, they become a שהכל. The הלכות to follow are only true when dealing with the 5 grains as flour.

4. **RULE #1:** The first rule we must know is: כל שיש בו מחמשת המינים מברכין עליו בורא מיני מזונות. This means: The ה' מינים, which are חשוב, that are mixed into a mixture of ingredients overpower the mixture and the ברכה will be a מזונות even if they are not the majority of the mixture. Normally, when you have a combination of foods eaten as one, the one that is the רוב/majority wins. However, this is not true when it comes to the ה' מינים. Since it is חשוב, it wins even if it's not the רוב. (סימן רח, סעיף ב')

5. **NOTE:** The previous הלכה is only true for the ברכה ראשונה; however, regarding making על המחיה, you only make one if you eat a כזית of the **actual** ה' מינים within 3–9 minutes. The other ingredients do not count towards the על המחיה. So, it can occur that you will have to make a בורא נפשות and מזונות on a food. (שם מ'ב ס'ק מח')

6. **RULE #2 - FLOUR ADDED NOT FOR TASTE:** If the flour of the ה' מינים is not added into a mixture for its taste, and it is only added for other reasons, it doesn't automatically win. Included in this is: (שם סעי' ב' וג)
   a. If it is added for texture, like to make it creamier or thicker
   b. If it is added for color
   c. If it is added to spread the food

7. Some examples are:
   a. Flour in licorice, which is only to give it texture
   b. Flour in soup is usually added to thicken it.
   c. Breadcrumbs added into tuna to make it creamier or to spread it (Breadcrumbs are cheaper than tuna.)

8. **RULE #3 – מזונות ADDED IN AN INSIGNIFICANT WAY:**

When מזונות is used as a coating or topping and it's thin, it can become a טפל and it won't automatically win. For example:

   a. Schnitzel with a thin coating of breadcrumbs is a שהכל because the main food is the chicken and the thin coating becomes טפל to the chicken. (If it has a thick coating then it is done so for taste and would perhaps be only a מזונות, and some say to make two ברכות on two other foods.) (זאת הברכה page 108-ג')

   b. Éclair ice cream bar that has a thin topping of מזונות crumbs is a שהכל since the thin coating of crumbs become טפל to the ice cream.

INGREDIENTS\ CEREALS\SNACKS

CHAPTER X

הלכות ברכות

1. To properly determine the ברכה for a particular cereal or snack, you must first know the ingredients and also know some basic facts:

    a. Any flour from the ה' מינים will make the cereal מזונות if it is there for taste.

    b. Rice flour is a מזונות. (סי' רח' סע' ז')

    c. Corn flour or corn meal is a שהכל since it is totally ground up and not recognizable as corn anymore.

    d. Bean flour, almond flour, or flour made from other grain (besides the ה' מינים) is שהכל.

    e. Wheat starch is only put in for texture.

    f. Pure bran is a שהכל.

    g. Wheat flakes are מזונות.

    h. Rolled grains mean the grains used in that product are whole and intact.

    i. Whole grain doesn't mean the grains are whole, but rather only that they use the whole kernel.

    j. Puffed grains are a האדמה since they are whole and intact. Intact grains from the ground are a האדמה.

    k. Any pureed fruit/vegetable/food with no recognizable pieces is a שהכל.

2. **HOW TO DETERMINE IF FLOUR IS ADDED FOR TASTE:**

    a. If the flour is first on the list, you know for sure that it is in there for taste, and if it is flour from the ה' מינים then you make a מזונות, even if it is not the majority in the entire mixture.

    b. If it is the second or third ingredient, sometimes it is there for taste and sometimes for texture, and research and/or logic is needed. Sometimes it is obvious from the product why the flour is in there.

    c. Anything past the third ingredient is only there for texture and will be בטל.

3. Usually, the order of ingredients listed on the label is an indication of the largest amount to the smallest. Here are some examples to explain the significance of this fact:

   a. If wheat flour is listed first, it is in there for taste and that food is automatically a מזונות even if the flour is not the רוב.

   b. If corn flour is listed first, that food will be a שהכל because corn flour is a שהכל, and most of the other ingredients are probably also שהכל. Since there is no ה' מינים in the ingredients, the ingredients that are רוב decide the ברכה.

   c. If rice flour is listed first, it is most likely a מזונות since rice flour is a מזונות and all the rest of the ingredients are likely there to enhance the rice. The rest of the ingredients must be checked to see if this is so. (Some have a מנהג to make a שהכל on rice flour.)

4. Following is a list of some foods that we will use as examples to explain why they have their particular ברכה:

   a. **Kellogg's Cornflakes**
   b. **Kemach cornflakes**
   c. **Rice Krispies**
   d. **Fruity Pebbles**
   e. **Crispix**
   f. **Puffed wheat**
   g. **Post Golden Crisp**
   h. **Kellogg's Sugar Smacks**
   i. **Corn Chex**
   j. **Rice/Chocolate Chex**
   k. **Corn chips**
   l. **Dipsy Doodles**
   m. **Tortilla chips**
   n. **Potato chips**

5. **CORNFLAKES:** Cornflakes can be made in one of two ways. One way is by grinding up the corn and making a batter out of it and then flaking the batter. Cornflakes made this way are a שהכל since the corn was ground up. The second way it can be made is by just flattening out the kernels of corn, which is a האדמה, since the kernels are still intact even though they are in a different shape. Kellogg's makes theirs in the second way so it's a האדמה. Kemach makes their cornflakes using corn flour (look on the box.) If you don't know which way a particular company makes it, you can just make a שהכל.

71

6. **RICE KRISPIES** and **FRUITY PEBBLES:** These are both made from rice flour and are cooked; the proper ברכה is a מזונות and a בורא נפשות.

7. **CRISPIX:** Crispix is one side of rice (the faded side) and the other side corn (the brighter side). Both are made from flour. The corn side is a שהכל and the rice side is a מזונות. Which ברכה should one make? Since they are exactly even and the מזונות is not from the ה' מינים, one should split them in half and make two ברכות.

8. **PUFFED WHEAT, POST GOLDEN CRISP,** and **KELLOGGS SUGAR SMACKS:** These cereals are all made by puffing them through intense heat and no cooking. They are therefore a האדמה because they are a whole grain, just in a different form.

9. **CORN CHEX:** This is a שהכל because it is made from ground corn. How do you know the corn is ground? Use your intellect to see that there are no whole pieces of corn in a piece of Chex.

10. **RICE/CHOCOLATE CHEX:** They are both מזונות since they are made from rice flour. Always check the ingredients to see what the ingredients are to determine the proper ברכה. Wheat Chex is made from wheat flour and is a מזונות. Vanilla Chex is made from rice, so it is מזונות. Honey-nut Chex is made from corn flour and is a שהכל.

11. **CORN CHIPS, DIPSY DOODLES,** and **TORTILLA CHIPS:** These are all שהכל since they are made from corn flour or milled corn. Use your intellect to see that they are made in a specific shape and would not look the way they do if they had actual pieces of corn.

12. **POTATO CHIPS:** Potato chip are האדמה since they are made from actual slices of potatoes. Pringles are made from potato flour — their shape proves it — and are a שהכל. Bamba is made from ground corn and is a שהכל.

13. **DRIZZILICIOUS:** These are rice cakes made mainly from rice flour and they require a מזונות. This company also makes popcorn which of course is a האדמה.

14. **ברכה אחרונה ON CEREAL:** The ברכה אחרונה on cereal depends on the ברכה ראשונה. If the ברכה on a cereal is מזונות because it's from the ה' מינים, then the ברכה אחרונה will only be על המחיה if you eat a כזית of the wheat. The כזית cannot include the other ingredients. Usually in a **full** bowl of cereal, you will have a כזית. (זאת הברכה פרק כב' ג', ד')

WHOLE GRAINS

CHAPTER XI

הלכות ברכות

CHAPTER XI – הלכות ברכות
WHOLE GRAINS

1. Even though on flour made from the ה' מינים you make a מזונות, on whole intact grains you make a האדמה. (ד' סעי' רח' סי')

2. The previous הלכה is only true if the grain tastes good and if it wasn't cooked. If it is cooked, it is a מזונות. If it is raw and tastes good or if it is baked or roasted and not stuck together, it is a האדמה. (א' סעי' שם)

3. **OATMEAL:** If you cook oats, it is a מזונות. Even if you soak oats in water or milk and it gets mushy and sticks together like when cooked, it is a מזונות. (Hot cereal, like farina, which is made from wheat flour, is a מזונות.)

4. **GRANOLA:** Granola is made from oats. There are different opinions as to what ברכה granola is, including a granola bar. Some say it is a האדמה since it is not cooked, and only baked. There are whole pieces, and they stick together only because of the honey and maple syrup mixed in. Some say that since it is baked in an oven and it is stuck together a little because of the baking, it is like it is cooked and it is a מזונות. One can't go wrong with either choice. However, you will have to be consistent when it comes to the ברכה אחרונה. See next הלכה.

5. **ברכה אחרונה ON GRANOLA:**
   a. If you make a מזונות on granola and you eat a כזית בכדי אכילת פרס (which is within four minutes), you will have to make על המחיה.

   b. If you make a האדמה on granola, you have an issue with the ברכה אחרונה. Some say you can just make a בורא נפשות; however, some say you should only eat it after washing on bread. Since there is a dispute, one should avoid this by eating less than a כזית of the granola within four minutes. One bar of a granola bar is less than a כזית. If you did eat more than a כזית within four minutes, you should just make a בורא נפשות. (ד' סעי' רח' סי')

6. **KIND BARS:** There are 3 types:
   a. Nuts Kind Bar – the ברכה depends on what's in the mixture. It is decided by the רוב.
   b. Soft Kind bar – breakfast bar – is a מזונות. It is soft and that can only happen if the oats are cooked.
   c. A hard Kind bar – this has the same qualities as a granola bar (see the הלכות of a granola bar).

7. PUFFED GRAINS: Grains that are puffed (which is done by popping the grain through heat) are essentially whole and intact and are therefore a האדמה. Some examples are:
   a. Popcorn
   b. Sugar crisp cereal
   c. Puffed wheat/rice cereal
   d. Sugar Smacks cereal
   e. Rice cakes
   f. Wheat cakes
   g. Spelt cakes
   h. Buckwheat cakes

8. **RICE CAKES:** Some say to make a מזונות, reasoning that since it is all packed together, it is like it is cooked together. However, many say to make a האדמה since it is whole and wasn't actually cooked together. (וזאת הברכה page 106 – פריכיות אורז)

9. The ברכה אחרונה for rice cakes is a בורא נפשות. Other "cakes" that are from the ה' מינים have the same הלכה as granola.

GROUND FRUITS\FOODS

CHAPTER XII

הלכות ברכות

1. **PUREED FRUITS OR VEGETABLES:** A food that is finely pureed to the point that there are no pieces becomes a שהכל, since it lost the character of its original creation. (רמ'א רב סעי' ז) If after pureeing, some pieces are still recognizable in the mixture, one should make the appropriate ברכה.

2. Based on the previous הלכה the following foods are שהכל:
   a. Applesauce (finely ground apples)
   b. Smoothie (finely ground fruits)
   c. Techina (finely ground sesame seeds)
   d. Chummus (finely ground chickpeas)
   e. Pringles (finely ground potatoes)
   f. Tomato sauce (finely ground tomatoes)
   g. Blended vegetable soup (finely ground vegetables)

3. **EXCEPTION:** There are a few examples of foods that even after being pureed retain their original form, and some hold that they do not downgrade to a שהכל and one should make the appropriate ברכה. Some examples are: Potato kugel, mashed avocado, and eggplant. Some will make a האדמה/העץ on these foods even after they have been mashed, and some will make a שהכל. Ask your *rav*.

4. If you make a העץ or האדמה on a pureed fruit or vegetable, בדיעבד you are יוצא your ברכה. (מ'ב סי' רח'ס'ק מ')

BRACHOS LIST

הלכות ברכות

FOOD	ברכה	NOTES
Acai	העץ בורא נפשות	If it is pureed, it is a שהכל.
Acai bowl	------>	Depends on what the רוב is and if it is eaten as one mixture. If the acai is רוב and pureed, it's שהכל.
All-Bran cereal	מזונות על המחיה	
Almond butter	שהכל בורא נפשות	
Alpha Bits cereal	מזונות על המחיה	Main ingredient is wheat flour.
Arugula	האדמה בורא נפשות	
Alfalfa	שהכל בורא נפשות	Grows on cotton, not on the ground.
Almond	העץ בורא נפשות	
Almond, chocolate-coated	שהכל והעץ בורא נפשות	If you're eating it for both. If you're eating it mainly for chocolate or for almond, then only העץ or שהכל.
Almond, sugar-coated	-------> בורא נפשות	If coating is thick and like chocolate, it is the same as previous הלכה. If it is only a thin layer of sugar, you only make a העץ.
Almonds, ground	-------> בורא נפשות	If eaten to enhance another food — e.g., topping on ice cream — ברכה is only made on other food. If eaten on its own: if finely ground, make שהכל; if coarse and recognizable, העץ.
Antibiotics, bitter tasting	none	
Antibiotics, pleasant tasting	שהכל	
Apple	העץ בורא נפשות	
Apple cake	מזונות על המחיה	
Apple chips	העץ בורא נפשות	
Apple crumble	מזונות על המחיה	
Apple Jacks cereal	מזונות על המחיה	Main ingredient is wheat flour.

FOOD	ברכה	NOTES
Apple juice /cider	שהכל בורא נפשות	
Apple kugel	------> על המחיה/ בורא נפשות	If flour is added to give taste or to make the kugel more filling, it's מזונות. If flour is only added to bind, it's העץ.
Apple rings	העץ בורא נפשות	
Applesauce – chunky	העץ בורא נפשות	
Applesauce – smooth	שהכל בורא נפשות	Pieces are not recognizable. If you see pieces, make העץ.
Apple strudel	מזונות על המחיה	Even though majority is fruit, the flour added from the 5 grains is considered the עיקר.
Apple, baked	העץ בורא נפשות	Juice left in bowl doesn't require ברכה (Unless you drink it later).
Apricot	העץ בורא נפשות	
Arbis (chickpeas)	האדמה בורא נפשות	
Artichoke	האדמה בורא נפשות	Needs to be checked for insects.
Asparagus	האדמה בורא נפשות	Needs to be checked for insects.
Avocado	העץ בורא נפשות	If mixed into vegetable salad, the רוב will decide the ברכה.
Baby food	שהכל	Since it is generally pureed.
Bagel	המוציא ברכת המזון	
Bagel chips	מזונות על המחיה	It is hard and made initially for a snack.
Baked beans	האדמה בורא נפשות	
Baked beans with pieces of hot dog	האדמה בורא נפשות	If the beans are the רוב.
Baked potato	האדמה בורא נפשות	Even if there is cheese on it, the cheese is a טפל.
Baked ziti	מזונות על המחיה	

FOOD	ברכה	NOTES
Bamba	שהכל בורא נפשות	Main ingredient is corn flour.
Banana	האדמה בורא נפשות	Tree doesn't last from year to year so the ברכה is האדמה.
Banana chips	האדמה בורא נפשות	
Banana split	------> בורא נפשות	Since the banana is to enhance the flavor of the ice cream, the ice cream is the עיקר and no ברכה is made on the banana.
Banana, mashed	האדמה בורא נפשות	If pieces are recognizable; if not, then שהכל.
Barley	מזונות על המחיה	Only pearl barley; complete barley is האדמה.
Barley soup	מזונות על המחיה ---->	Even if barley is minority, since it is of the 5 grains, the ברכה follows the barley. If a כזית of barley was eaten within 4 min
Bean soup	האדמה בורא נפשות---->	If a כזית of beans was eaten within 4 min
Bean sprouts	שהכל בורא נפשות	Grows with water on cotton, not from the ground.
Beef	שהכל בורא נפשות	
Beef burger	שהכל בורא נפשות	
Beef jerky	שהכל בורא נפשות	
Beer	שהכל בורא נפשות	
Beet juice	שהכל בורא נפשות	
Beets	האדמה בורא נפשות	
Biscuits	מזונות על המחיה	
Bissli	מזונות על המחיה	
Blintzes	מזונות על המחיה	
Blondies	מזונות על המחיה	
Blueberries	העץ בורא נפשות	If they are from a bush above 9 inches. Wild blueberries from a bush below 9 inches are האדמה. Some say it has scale insects.
Blueberry pie	מזונות על המחיה/ בורא נפשות	If the crust is very thin, then make a ברכה on the blueberries.

FOOD	ברכה	NOTES
Borekas	מזונות על המחיה	
Borscht	האדמה בורא נפשות	
Boston cream pie	מזונות על המחיה	
Bourbon	שהכל	
Bran (pure)	שהכל בורא נפשות	Made from outer shell of grain which is a מאכל בהמה.
Bran flakes	מזונות על המחיה	Main ingredient is wheat flour.
Brandy	שהכל	
Bread	המוציא ברכת המזון	
Bread rolls	המוציא ברכת המזון	
Bread sticks	מזונות על המחיה	
Breaded eggplant	------> בורא נפשות/על המחיה	If it is a thick coating, make מזונות; if it is a thin coating, make האדמה.
Broccoli	האדמה בורא נפשות	Needs to be checked for insects.
Broccoli kugel	------> בורא נפשות	If made with recognizable pieces, it's האדמה; if not recognizable, it's שהכל.
Brownies Brownie bars	מזונות על המחיה	
Brussels sprouts	האדמה בורא נפשות	Needs to be checked for insects.
Buckwheat	האדמה בורא נפשות	It is a grain.
Buckwheat cakes	האדמה בורא נפשות	It is puffed grain.
Butter	שהכל	
Butter cookies	מזונות על המחיה	
Cabbage	האדמה בורא נפשות	Needs to be checked for insects.
Cabbage soup	האדמה בורא נפשות---->	If pieces of cabbage are recognizable. If it is pureed, it's שהכל. If a כזית of cabbage was eaten within 4 min
Cake batter	שהכל	

FOOD	ברכה	NOTES
Calzone	מזונות על המחיה	If it's a meal-type food (it's big) then it's like pizza, but if it's a snack-type food (it's small) it's מזונות.
Cantaloupe	האדמה בורא נפשות	
Cap'n Crunch cereal	שהכל בורא נפשות	Main ingredient is corn flour.
Carob/buksar	העץ בורא נפשות	Needs to be checked for insects.
Carrot & raisin salad	האדמה בורא נפשות	Since the raisins are the מיעוט, they are בטל. (Raisins – insects – ask your *rav*)
Carrot juice	שהכל בורא נפשות	
Carrots	האדמה בורא נפשות	
Carrot muffin	מזונות על המחיה/ בורא נפשות	It usually contains flour. If no flour is used and carrots are recognizable, it's האדמה; if not, it's שהכל.
Cashew nuts	העץ בורא נפשות	
Cauliflower	האדמה בורא נפשות	Needs to be checked for insects.
Celery	האדמה בורא נפשות	Needs to be checked for insects.
Celery juice	שהכל בורא נפשות	
Challah	המוציא ברכת המזון	
Challah kugel	מזונות על המחיה	It is usually made with mashed-up challah, and it is cooked or soaked, so it loses its שם לחם and is מזונות.
Champagne	הגפן על הגפן	
Cheerios	מזונות על המחיה	Main ingredient is oat flour.
Cheese	שהכל בורא נפשות	
Cheese blintzes	מזונות על המחיה	
Cheesecake	מזונות על המחיה	If the base is very thin and just to support the cheese and not for taste, then it is שהכל.
Cheese curls	שהכל בורא נפשות	
Cheese, grated	שהכל בורא נפשות	

FOOD	ברכה	NOTES
Cheese latkes	שהכל בורא נפשות	Flour is added only for texture. If there is a lot of flour, which is probably put in for taste, then it is a מזונות.
Cheese stick	מזונות על המחיה	Bread-like on outside with cheese inside.
Cherry	העץ בורא נפשות	
Cherry danish	מזונות על המחיה	
Cherry liqueur	שהכל	
Chestnuts, roasted	העץ בורא נפשות	Needs to be checked for insects.
Chex (corn, honey nut)	שהכל בורא נפשות	Always check ingredients of Chex cereal; if it's made from corn it's שהכל, but if it's made from rice or wheat it is מזונות.
Chex (wheat, rice, vanilla, chocolate)	מזונות על המחיה/ בורא נפשות	On rice flour you make a בורא נפשות.
Chia seeds	האדמה בורא נפשות	
Chicken	שהכל בורא נפשות	
Chicken coated with Rice Krispies, potato chips	שהכל בורא נפשות	The Rice Krispies and chips are only enhancing the chicken.
Chicken coated with pretzels	------> בורא נפשות/על המחיה	If the pretzels are a thick coating, make מזונות; if not, it is שהכל.
Chicken salad	שהכל בורא נפשות	When eaten as one combination and the chicken is the רוב ingredient. If רוב are vegetables, then האדמה.
Chicken soup – plain	שהכל ---->	No ברכה אחרונה. One did not drink a רביעית without a הפסק.
Chicken soup with kneidlach	מזונות/ שהכל על המחיה	מזונות on kneidlach, then שהכל on soup.
Chicken soup with vegetables	שהכל בורא נפשות<---->	When eaten mainly for soup and as one entity. If vegetables are eaten separately, they require a ברכה. If a כזית of vegetables was eaten within 4 min.
Chicken with stuffing	------> בורא נפשות/על המחיה	First make מזונות on stuffing, then שהכל and eat chicken w/o stuffing. Since a lot of chicken is eaten without the stuffing, it needs its own ברכה.
Chicken, Southern fried	------> בורא נפשות/על המחיה	If thick coating, it's מזונות; if thin coating, it's שהכל. If chicken is eaten separately, make two ברכות.
Chili	האדמה בורא נפשות	Assuming beans are the majority. If meat is majority, then it's שהכל.

FOOD	ברכה	NOTES
Chinese noodles	מזונות על המחיה	
Chocolate	שהכל בורא נפשות	
Chocolate cake	מזונות על המחיה	
Chocolate chips	שהכל בורא נפשות	
Chocolate-coated cookies	מזונות על המחיה	
Chocolate-covered strawberries	האדמה בורא נפשות	Strawberries contain insects.
Chocolate-coated wafer	מזונות על המחיה	
Chocolate lentils	שהכל בורא נפשות	
Chocolate milk	שהכל בורא נפשות	
Chocolate orange peels	שהכל בורא נפשות	Since orange peels are not the real fruit their ברכה is שהכל. Orange peels may have insects.
Chocolate with Rice Krispies	שהכל בורא נפשות	Rice Krispies are בטל to the chocolate.
Chocolate bar with almonds	שהכל בורא נפשות	Since the main objective is the chocolate.
Chocolate bar with nuts	שהכל בורא נפשות	Since the main objective is the chocolate.
Chopped liver	שהכל בורא נפשות	
Chow mein (rice and chicken)	-------> בורא נפשות	If רוב is rice, make מזונות; if רוב is chicken, make שהכל.
Chow mein noodles	מזונות על המחיה	
Cholent - beans, meat, potatoes	-------> בורא נפשות	ברכה is made on whatever is רוב when eaten together on one spoon.
Cholent - containing barley	מזונות על המחיה	Due to barley content and when eaten as a mixture all at once on each spoonful.
Chummus	שהכל בורא נפשות	
Cider	שהכל בורא נפשות	
Cinnamon Toast Crunch cereal	מזונות על המחיה	Main ingredient is wheat flour.
Clementine	העץ בורא נפשות	

FOOD	ברכה	NOTES
Coca-Cola	שהכל בורא נפשות	
Cocktail sausages	שהכל בורא נפשות	
Cocoa Pebbles cereal	מזונות בורא נפשות	Main ingredient is rice flour. The ברכה אחרונה is בורא נפשות.
Cocoa	שהכל	
Cocoa Puffs cereal	שהכל בורא נפשות	Main ingredient is corn flour.
Coconut	העץ בורא נפשות	
Coconut milk	שהכל בורא נפשות	
Coffee	שהכל	No ברכה אחרונה since it is not consumed fast enough.
Cognac	שהכל בורא נפשות	Originally from wine but it is distilled so it is a שהכל.
Cole slaw	האדמה בורא נפשות	
Cookies (From ה' מינים)	מזונות על המחיה	
Cookie Crisp cereal	שהכל בורא נפשות	Main ingredient is corn flour.
Corn cakes	האדמה בורא נפשות	It is made from puffed corn which is האדמה.
Corn chips	שהכל בורא נפשות	It is made from corn flour.
Corn dogs	מזונות על המחיה	The batter contains flour that is for taste.
Cookie dough	-----> בורא נפשות/על המחיה	שהכל since it's not being eaten in normal way. Perhaps nowadays it is normal, and then it is a מזונות.
Cornflakes (Kellogg's)	האדמה בורא נפשות	Pressed corn kernel. Since corn is whole and just pressed it retains its האדמה. If a brand uses corn flour, its cornflakes are שהכל. (Kemach uses corn flour = שהכל)
Corn muffin	מזונות על המחיה/בורא נפשות	It contains flour. If no flour is used, then שהכל.
Corn nuts	האדמה בורא נפשות	
Corn on the cob	האדמה בורא נפשות	Needs to be checked for insects.

FOOD	ברכה	NOTES
Corn pops	שהכל בורא נפשות	It is made from corn flour.
Corned beef	שהכל בורא נפשות	
Cottage cheese	שהכל בורא נפשות	
Cotton candy	שהכל בורא נפשות	
Cough drops	שהכל	They taste good.
Couscous	מזונות על המחיה	
Cracker with tuna	מזונות ושהכל בורא נפשות/על המחיה	
Crackers	מזונות על המחיה	
Craisins	האדמה בורא נפשות	Dried cranberries. Plant grows very low to ground. Some say to make העץ.
Cranberry	האדמה בורא נפשות	Plant grows very low to ground. Some say to make העץ.
Cranberry juice	שהכל בורא נפשות	
Cream	שהכל בורא נפשות	
Cream-filled cupcake	מזונות על המחיה	
Cream with fruit	------> בורא נפשות	If the fruit is the main food, make העץ, if the cream is the main part, make שהכל.
Crembo	------> על המחיה/בורא נפשות	If there is a cookie on bottom and you eat it with the cream, make one ברכה of מזונות. If you eat the cream separately, add שהכל.
Crepes	מזונות על המחיה	
Crispix cereal	------> בורא נפשות	Is exactly half rice flour and half corn flour, so there's no רוב. Split it in half and make 2 ברכות: שהכל on yellow side and מזונות on the other.
Croutons – made from bread	------>	If pieces are smaller than a כזית and boiled or deep fried, make מזונות; if not, make המוציא.
Croutons – small yellow	מזונות על המחיה	
Cucumber	האדמה בורא נפשות	

FOOD	ברכה	NOTES
Cucumber salad	האדמה בורא נפשות	
Cupcake	מזונות על המחיה	
Currants	העץ בורא נפשות	
Date	העץ על העץ	
Deli roll	מזונות על המחיה	
Doritos	שהכל בורא נפשות	Made from ground corn.
Doughnut	מזונות על המחיה	
Doughnut dipped in coffee	מזונות על המחיה	The מנהג seems to be not to have to wash hands before doing so, although some say to wash.
Dried banana	האדמה בורא נפשות	
Dried mango	העץ בורא נפשות	
Dried papaya	האדמה בורא נפשות	ברכה is unclear. Best to פטור by making העץ and האדמה on other foods.
Dried peach	העץ בורא נפשות	
Drizzilicious (Little rice cakes) If it is popcorn, then it is האדמה.	מזונות בורא נפשות	Main ingredient is rice flour, which is מזונות. Some chassidim hold that you make שהכל on rice flour.
Duck	שהכל בורא נפשות	
Éclair (Custard filling)	מזונות על המחיה	
Éclair ice cream	שהכל ------>	Mainly ice cream with thin crumb topping. Ice cream is not consumed fast enough to make a בורא נפשות.
Edemame	האדמה בורא נפשות	
Egg	שהכל בורא נפשות	
Egg matzoh	מזונות על המחיה	If you are קובע סעודה, it is המוציא.
Egg omelet	שהכל בורא נפשות	
Egg roll	מזונות על המחיה	
Egg salad	שהכל בורא נפשות	

FOOD	ברכה	NOTES
Eggplant	האדמה בורא נפשות	
Eggplant parmesan	האדמה בורא נפשות	The sauce and cheese only enhance the eggplant.
Eggplant spread	שהכל בורא נפשות	Since it is totally pureed.
Eggs with vegetables	------> בורא נפשות	If eggs are to enhance vegetables, make האדמה; if vegetables are to enhance eggs, make שהכל.
Egozi bar (chocolate)	שהכל בורא נפשות	Made of chocolate and nougat and some nuts.
Empanada	מזונות על המחיה	
Enchilada chips	שהכל בורא נפשות	Made from corn flour.
Encore	מזונות על המחיה	
Esrog	------> בורא נפשות	Raw; since not דרך to eat, ברכה is שהכל.
Esrog jam	העץ	Because pieces are recognizable.
Falafel (pita bread)	המוציא ברכת המזון	
Falafel balls	------> בורא נפשות/על המחיה	שהכל - If made from finely ground chickpeas, and no flour for taste. מזונות – If flour is added for taste. האדמה – If no flour for taste and there are still pieces of chickpeas.
Farfel	מזונות על המחיה	
Farina	מזונות על המחיה	Made from wheat flour.
Fiber One cereal	מזונות על המחיה	Main ingredient is wheat flour.
Fig	העץ על העץ	Needs to be checked for insects.
Fig bar	מזונות על המחיה	
Fish balls	שהכל בורא נפשות	
Fish cakes	שהכל בורא נפשות	Matzoh meal is added for binding purposes.
Fish sticks	-------> בורא נפשות/על המחיה	Depends on thickness of coating; see fried fish.
Flavored vitamins	שהכל	

FOOD	ברכה	NOTES
Flax seeds	האדמה בורא נפשות	
Flutes	שהכל בורא נפשות	Main ingredient is corn flour.
Franks 'n blanks	מזונות על המחיה	If you eat a כזית of the dough.
French fries	האדמה בורא נפשות	Even if some flour is added, it is only as a binder or as a thin coating.
French toast	המוציא ברכת המזון	
French Toast Crunch cereal	שהכל בורא נפשות	Main ingredient is corn flour.
Fried fish	------ > על המחיה/בורא נפשות	Thick coating – מזונות' thin coating - שהכל.
Frosted Flakes cereal	האדמה בורא נפשות	Only for Kellogg's or any company that uses whole pieces of corn.
Frosties cereal	האדמה בורא נפשות	Made from pressed corn.
Fruit & Fibre cereal	מזונות על המחיה	
Fruit cocktail	------ > בורא נפשות/על העץ	If mostly העץ, then all is העץ; if mostly האדמה, then all is האדמה. If you eat fruits separately, make 2 ברכות.
Fruit Loops cereal	מזונות על המחיה	Main ingredient is wheat flour.
Fruit roll ups	שהכל בורא נפשות	
Fruit leather	שהכל בורא נפשות	
Fruit soup	------ > בורא נפשות/על העץ	With pieces, make ברכה of main fruits; without pieces, it's שהכל.
Fruity Pebbles cereal	מזונות בורא נפשות	Main ingredient is rice flour. The ברכה אחרונה is a בורא נפשות.
Garlic bread	המוציא ברכת המזון	Made to eat as a meal.
Garlic knots	------ >	See Chapter VIII #21.i
Garlic soft pretzels	------ >	See Chapter VIII #21.i
Garlic, raw	שהכל	Not the דרך to eat.
Garlic, roasted, baked	האדמה בורא נפשות	
Gefilte fish	שהכל בורא נפשות	The flour that is added is only to help bind it together.

FOOD	ברכה	NOTES
Ginger	שהכל	Not the דרך to eat.
Ginger ale	שהכל בורא נפשות	
Gingerbread man	מזונות על המחיה	
Gogo squeeze	שהכל בורא נפשות	
Golden Crisp cereal	האדמה ------>	It is a puffed whole grain, which is האדמה. For ברכה אחרונה look at buckwheat cakes.
Goulash (meat and potatoes)	שהכל בורא נפשות	If רוב is meat. If the רוב is potatoes, you make a האדמה. If eaten separately, make two ברכות.
Grab1 nutrition bar	שהכל בורא נפשות	
Graham crackers	מזונות על המחיה	
Granola	------> ------>	Each brand may be different. If oats are cooked first, they are a מזונות; however, if they are only baked, it's a מחלוקת. Some say it's האדמה and some say it's מזונות. Ask your *rav*. See Granola bars.
Granola bars	------> ------>	Same as granola. If you make a מזונות then you make על המחיה. If you make a האדמה, it's best not to eat a כזית within 4 minutes. One bar is less than a כזית. If you did eat a כזית within 4 minutes, make a בורא נפשות.
Grapes	העץ על העץ	Needs to be checked for insects.
Grape juice	הגפן על הגפן	
Grape juice with seltzer	------> (If you drink a רביעית of grape juice first, then על הגפן. If you drink the diluted grape juice, בורא נפשות	One should not make a ברכה even on minimally diluted grape juice; instead, make ברכה on full grape juice (and preferably drink a רביעית). (Rabbi Falk)
Grape soda	שהכל בורא נפשות	Artificial flavoring.
Grapefruit	העץ בורא נפשות	
Grapefruit juice	שהכל בורא נפשות	
Green beans	האדמה בורא נפשות	
Green pepper	האדמה בורא נפשות	
Grilled cheese sandwich	המוציא ברכת המזון	

FOOD	ברכה	NOTES
Guacamole	העץ בורא נפשות	Unless it is totally pureed; then it is שהכל.
Guava	העץ בורא נפשות	Unless it is dried; then it is שהכל since it is totally pureed.
Gum	שהכל	
Gummy bears	שהכל בורא נפשות	
Gushers	שהכל בורא נפשות	
Halvah	שהכל בורא נפשות	
Hamburger with bun	המוציא ברכת המזון	
Hamburger without bun	שהכל בורא נפשות	Even if flour is added, it is only to bind or soften.
Hazelnut	העץ בורא נפשות	
Hazelnut butter	שהכל	
Hearts of palm	------> בורא נפשות	מחלוקת. Either האדמה or העץ. Either one is fine.
Herbal tea	שהכל	No ברכה אחרונה since it is not consumed fast enough.
Herring	שהכל בורא נפשות	
Herring on crackers	מזונות and שהכל בורא נפשות/על המחיה	Since you want both and it's not a mixture, only one on top of the other.
Hamantashen	מזונות על המחיה	
Honey	שהכל	No ברכה אחרונה since it is not consumed fast enough.
Honey Bunches of Oats cereal	מזונות על המחיה	Main ingredient is wheat flour.
Honey cake	מזונות על המחיה	
Honeycomb cereal	מזונות על המחיה	Main ingredient is wheat flour.
Honeydew	האדמה בורא נפשות	
Honey Nut Cheerios cereal	מזונות על המחיה	Main ingredient is wheat flour.
Honey Smacks cereal	האדמה ------>	Whole puffed grains. For ברכה אחרונה see buckwheat cakes.

FOOD	ברכה	NOTES
Horseradish	שהכל	
Hot chocolate	שהכל	No ברכה אחרונה since you can't drink a רביעית fast enough.
Hot dogs	שהכל בורא נפשות	
Hot peppers	האדמה בורא נפשות	
Ice cream	שהכל ------>	No ברכה אחרונה since it has a הלכה like a liquid and you cannot eat a רביעית fast enough.
Ice cream cone	מזונות על המחיה	
Ice cream in cone	------> (If cone is eaten fast enough – על המחיה)	If cone is plain and is basically in place of cup, it does not require ברכה even when ice cream is finished. A flavored cone, or if one likes the plain one, requires a separate ברכה of מזונות.
Ice cream sandwich	------> (If cookie is eaten fast enough, על המחיה)	Make מזונות on wafer on its own, then eat a little ice cream on its own and make שהכל.
Ice cream with pieces of nuts	שהכל	
Ice cream with topping	שהכל	Even if topping is מזונות.
Iced coffee	שהכל בורא נפשות unless sipped slowly	
Iced tea	שהכל בורא נפשות unless sipped slowly	
Ices (Including alcoholic ices)	שהכל	No ברכה אחרונה since it is not consumed fast enough.
Instant potatoes	שהכל בורא נפשות	Some say האדמה.
Jalapeno chips	האדמה בורא נפשות	Made from real slices of potatoes.
Jam	שהכל	Without fruit pieces.
Jello	שהכל בורא נפשות	
Jelly	שהכל	
Jellybeans	שהכל בורא נפשות	
Jelly rings	שהכל בורא נפשות	
Jolly ranchers	שהכל בורא נפשות	

FOOD	ברכה	NOTES
Juice of canned fruit	שהכל בורא נפשות	If you drink it by itself. If you eat pieces of fruit as well, העץ covers fruit and juice.
Kale	האדמה בורא נפשות	Is heavily infested.
Kale chips	האדמה בורא נפשות	If made from real kale. If made artificially it could be שהכל.
Kani	שהכל בורא נפשות	
Kasha (buckwheat)	האדמה בורא נפשות	
Ketchup	שהכל	
Kibbeh	מזונות על המחיה	
Kidney beans	האדמה בורא נפשות	
Kif Kaf	מזונות על המחיה	Wafer inside.
Kishke	מזונות על המחיה	
Kiwi	העץ בורא נפשות	
Kix (cereal)	שהכל בורא נפשות	Main ingredient is corn flour.
Kind bars	------> על המחיה / look at granola	If it is a soft bar it is מזונות and על המחיה. If it is the hard bar, then it is like a granola bar.
Klik bars	------>	Many different types: Depends on what is on the inside — a wafer, rice, or just chocolate — and you must determine what is the רוב.
Kneidlach	מזונות על המחיה	Even if eaten together with chicken soup. See chicken soup.
Knish	מזונות על המחיה	
Kohlrabi	האדמה בורא נפשות	
Kremsel - crushed matzo with egg	מזונות על המחיה	
Kreplach	מזונות על המחיה	Main ingredient is wheat flour.
Lace cookies	------> בורא נפשות/עלהמחיה	If made without any flour, it's שהכל. If flour is added for taste, it's מזונות.
Lachmagine	מזונות על המחיה	

FOOD	ברכה	NOTES
Lady fingers	שהכל בורא נפשות	Contains no flour.
Laffy Taffy	שהכל בורא נפשות	
Lahit	מזונות על המחיה	Wafer inside.
Lamb chops	שהכל בורא נפשות	
Lasagna	מזונות על המחיה	
Lasso laces	שהכל בורא נפשות	
L'chaim	שהכל בורא נפשות	
Leek	האדמה בורא נפשות	
Lemon	שהכל	Not the דרך to eat.
Lemon juice	שהכל בורא נפשות	
Lemonade	שהכל בורא נפשות	
Lentil soup	האדמה בורא נפשות	If pieces are recognizable. If pureed, it's שהכל.
Lentils (cooked)	האדמה בורא נפשות	
Lettuce	האדמה בורא נפשות	Needs to be checked for insects.
Licorice	שהכל בורא נפשות	Flour in it is for binding purposes.
Licorice root	שהכל	Because only the flavor is eaten, not actual root.
Life cereal	מזונות על המחיה	Main ingredient is wheat flour.
Liver	שהכל בורא נפשות	
Lokshen	מזונות על המחיה	
Lollipop	שהכל	No ברכה אחרונה since it is not consumed fast enough.
London broil	שהכל בורא נפשות	
Lotus cream	שהכל בורא נפשות	

FOOD	ברכה	NOTES
Lox	שהכל בורא נפשות	
Lychee	העץ בורא נפשות	
Macadamia nuts	העץ בורא נפשות	
Macaroni	מזונות על המחיה	
Macaroni & cheese	מזונות על המחיה	
Macaroons	שהכל בורא נפשות	
Mandarins	העץ בורא נפשות	
Mango	העץ בורא נפשות	
Mango nectar	שהכל בורא נפשות	
Margarine	שהכל	
Marshmallows (Marshmallow fluff)	שהכל בורא נפשות	Often made with fish gelatin. Mouth needs to be washed out after fleishigs (ex: barbecue).
Marzipan	שהכל בורא נפשות	
Matzo meal cake	מזונות על המחיה	
Matzoh	המוציא ברכת המזון	
Matzoh brie	מזונות על המחיה	Since pieces are less than a כזית and it is soaked in water which removes its appearance of bread.
Matzoh cracker	מזונות על המחיה	It is hard and made for a snack.
Meat & vegetable stew	-------> בורא נפשות	Make ברכה only on רוב if you are eating them together as one.
Meat and potato pie	-------> נפשות	Make ברכה only on רוב.
Meatloaf	שהכל בורא נפשות	Flour is only added to bind.
Meatballs	שהכל בורא נפשות	
Meatballs & spaghetti	---–-> בורא נפשות/על המחיה	If meatballs are eaten separately, make 2 ברכות; if eaten together, make only מזונות.
Medicine	------->	If unflavored, no ברכה. If flavored, better to first make שהכל on something else (aside from water).

FOOD	ברכה	NOTES
Medicine with <u>juice</u> in order to take	שהכל בורא נפשות	
Medicine with <u>water</u> in order to take	none	
Melba toast	מזונות על המחיה	They are hard and made initially for a snack.
Melon	האדמה בורא נפשות	
Meringue	שהכל בורא נפשות	
'Mezonos bread'	------->	Consult your *rav*. (Many hold that you must wash!)
Mike and Ikes	שהכל בורא נפשות	
Milk	שהכל בורא נפשות	
Milk left in cereal Bowl	none	בטל to cereal if you drink it straight after eating. (Unless you added a lot of milk having in mind to drink it after)
Milk Munch	שהכל בורא נפשות	
Milk shake	שהכל בורא נפשות	
Mints	שהכל בורא נפשות	
Mozzarella sticks	שהכל בורא נפשות	Mainly cheese with a little breading on top.
Mouthwash strips	None	Not considered food.
Mouthwash	None	Not considered food.
Muddy buddies made with a mixture of Chex.	-----> על המחיה/בורא נפשות	If eaten separately, you need the appropriate ברכה. When eaten as a mixture, if there is Wheat Chex in it, make מזונות. If it's mixture of שהכל Chex and מזונות Chex (not wheat), the ברכה is decided by the רוב. See Chex to know which ברכות to make on each.
Muesli	מזונות על המחיה Look at granola	Only if oatmeal is cooked. If it is raw, make האדמה.
Multi-grain bread	המוציא ברכת המזון	
Mushroom	שהכל בורא נפשות	Grows from moisture, not the ground.

FOOD	ברכה	NOTES
Mushroom & barley soup	מזונות If you eat a כזית of barley within 4 min – על המחיה ----<>	Since barley is from ה' מינים it wins over all other ingredients when eaten as a mixture. If you eat the mushrooms separately, make a שהכל, too, and if you eat a כזית within 4 min., besides the על המחיה make בורא נפשות.
Mushroom soup	שהכל בורא נפשות----<>	If you eat a כזית of mushrooms within 4 minutes.
Mustard	שהכל	
Napoleon	מזונות על המחיה	
Nectarine	העץ בורא נפשות	
Noodle kugel	מזונות על המחיה	
Noodle soup	מזונות על המחיה----<>	Since it is mainly noodles. If you eat a כזית of noodles within 4 min.
Nougat	שהכל בורא נפשות	
NuGo bar	שהכל בורא נפשות	
Nutella	שהכל בורא נפשות	
Nutty chews	שהכל בורא נפשות	If you are eating it for the peanuts, make האדמה.
Oatmeal	מזונות על המחיה/ Look at granola	Only cooked oatmeal. If it is raw, it's האדמה.
Oatmeal cookies	מזונות על המחיה See granola	If made with flour for taste. If there is no flour or only a little for binding purposes, then it is the same as granola.
Olives, black	העץ על העץ	
Olives, green	העץ על העץ	
Olives with red stuffing	העץ על העץ	
Omelet	שהכל בורא נפשות	
Onion rolls	המוציא ברכת המזון	
Onion rings	מזונות על המחיה	Battered, dipped onions with a thick coating. If it has a thin coating, then it is a האדמה. Some have pureed onions inside and then it's a מזונות, even with a thin coating.
Onion rings snack	שהכל בורא נפשות	It is made from corn flour.
Onion soup	------<> בורא נפשות----<>	If thick from sautéed onions, make האדמה; if from soup mix, make שהכל. If you eat a כזית of onions within 4 minutes.

FOOD	ברכה	NOTES
Onion, fried	האדמה בורא נפשות	
Onion, raw	שהכל בורא נפשות	Not the דרך to be eaten raw.
Orange	העץ בורא נפשות	
Orange juice	שהכל בורא נפשות	
Orange peel	------> בורא נפשות	If no flavor, no ברכה; if there is a flavor, make שהכל as it is not main פרי. (May have insects)
Orzo	מזונות על המחיה	
Pomelo	העץ בורא נפשות	
Pancakes	מזונות על המחיה	
Papaya	האדמה בורא נפשות	ברכה is unclear as it has qualities of a vegetable and fruit. Best is to פטור it by making העץ and האדמה on other foods. If no option, ברכה is האדמה.
Parsley	שהכל	Not the דרך to be eaten. Needs to be checked for insects.
Parsnip	האדמה בורא נפשות	
Passionfruit	העץ בורא נפשות	
Pastrami	שהכל בורא נפשות	
Pea soup	האדמה בורא נפשות---->	If pieces are recognizable. If pureed, make שהכל. If you eat a כזית of peas within 4 minutes.
Peach	העץ בורא נפשות	
Peach pie	מזונות על המחיה/ בורא נפשות	If the crust is very thin, make העץ.
Peaches & cream	העץ בורא נפשות	With the assumption you are eating it for the peaches and the cream is enhancing it.
Peanut butter-filled Pretzels	מזונות על המחיה	
Peanut butter Sandwich	המוציא ברכת המזון	
Peanut butter – smooth	שהכל בורא נפשות	
Peanut butter – crunchy	האדמה בורא נפשות	

FOOD	ברכה	NOTES
Peanut chews / nutty chews (Peanuts, caramel, chocolate)	שהכל בורא נפשות	If you eat it for the peanuts it would be האדמה.
Peanut chews (Rice Krispies & peanut butter)	מזונות בורא נפשות	
Peanuts	האדמה בורא נפשות	
Peanuts, chocolate-coated	האדמה בורא נפשות	If outside is first sucked, then 2 ברכות.
Peanuts, sugar-coated	------> בורא נפשות	If coating is hard and eaten before nut, make שהכל on coating, and before eating the nut make האדמה. If thin layer of sugar only האדמה.
Peanuts and raisins	------> ------>	If you eat them separately, make העץ and האדמה; if you're eating as a mixture, then whatever is רוב. If eaten separately, בורא נפשות and על העץ; if eaten together, the ברכה אחרונה decides your ברכה ראשונה.
Pears	העץ בורא נפשות	
Peas	האדמה בורא נפשות	
Pecans	העץ בורא נפשות	
Pecan pie	------> בורא נפשות/על המחיה	If the crust is very thin, make העץ on the pecans, but if the crust is thick, make מזונות.
Persimmon/ Sharon fruit	העץ בורא נפשות	
Pesach cake	------> בורא נפשות/על המחיה	Made w/ matzoh meal – מזונות. Made w/ potato flour – שהכל.
Pickles	האדמה בורא נפשות	
Pie	מזונות על המחיה/ בורא נפשות	Dough is the עיקר even if it is less than רוב, unless the crust is very thin.
Pineapple	האדמה בורא נפשות	Tree dies every year so ברכה is האדמה. (Check for insects.)
Pineapple juice	שהכל בורא נפשות	
Pistachio	העץ בורא נפשות	First make העץ and eat nut before sucking salt on shell.
Pita	המוציא ברכת המזון	
Pita chips	מזונות על המחיה	In most cases they are baked initially in chip form. If it is homemade from real pita, then it is המוציא unless it is smaller than a כזית and deep-fried. (See Chapter VIII #25.)

FOOD	ברכה	NOTES
Pizza	------> ברכת המזון/ על המחיה	Consult your *rav*. (Some say המוציא even for one bite. Some say מזונות unless you eat an amount of a meal.)
Pizza snaps	מזונות על המחיה	They are bread with a filling and made to eat as a snack.
Pizza sticks	מזונות על המחיה	They are bread with a filling made to eat as a snack.
Plantain chips	האדמה בורא נפשות	They're banana chips.
Plum	העץ בורא נפשות	
Poke bowl	-----> בורא נפשות	Depends on the רוב and if it is eaten as one entity or separately.
Pomegranate	העץ על העץ	
Popcorn	האדמה בורא נפשות	Even if flavored. (Drizzilicious makes flavored popcorn besides rice cakes.)
Potato	האדמה בורא נפשות	
Potato chips	האדמה בורא נפשות	
Potato knish	מזונות על המחיה	
Potato kugel	האדמה בורא נפשות	If pureed very finely some say שהכל.
Potato latkes	האדמה בורא נפשות	If pureed very finely some say שהכל.
Potato poppers	שהכל בורא נפשות	Made from corn flour.
Potato salad	האדמה בורא נפשות	
Potato taters	האדמה בורא נפשות	
Potato soup	האדמה בורא נפשות---->	If pieces are recognizable. If pureed, make שהכל. If a כזית of pieces of potatoes are eaten within 4 minutes.
Potatoes (cooked and mashed)	האדמה בורא נפשות	It is still a potato, just mashed up.
Potatoes, raw	שהכל	Since inedible to most people.
Pretzel – hard	מזונות על המחיה	
Pretzel rolls/buns	המוציא ברכת המזון	It is pure bread, just in the shape of a pretzel or bun, etc.

FOOD	ברכה	NOTES
Pretzel – soft	------>	See Chapter VIII #21.h
Pringles	שהכל בורא נפשות	Some hold האדמה.
Prune juice	שהכל בורא נפשות	
Prunes	העץ בורא נפשות	
P'tcha/gala	שהכל בורא נפשות	
Pudding	שהכל בורא נפשות	
Puffed pastry	מזונות על המחיה	
Puffed rice	האדמה בורא נפשות	If it is a rice cake, some say מזונות since it is pressed together.
Puffed wheat	האדמה ----->	If it is a rice cake, some say it is a מזונות. These are whole kernels from the ה' מינים and some say to only eat in a bread meal, and some say you make בורא נפשות. Either eat in a bread meal, or don't eat a כזית within 4 minutes. If you ate a כזית within 4 minutes not in a bread meal, make a בורא נפשות.
Puffins cereal	מזונות על המחיה	
Pumpernickel bread	המוציא ברכת המזון	
Pumpkin	האדמה בורא נפשות	
Pumpkin seeds	האדמה בורא נפשות	
Pureed fruit	שהכל בורא נפשות	Finely pureed foods downgrade to a שהכל. ברכה אחרונה only if you drank a רביעית straight.
Pureed soups	שהכל ------>	Finely pureed foods downgrade to a שהכל. No ברכה אחרונה is made if a רביעית was not consumed at once.
Quiche	מזונות על המחיה	
Quinoa	האדמה בורא נפשות	Needs to be checked for insects.
Radish	האדמה בורא נפשות	
Raisin bran	מזונות על המחיה	
Raisin bread	המוציא ברכת המזון	
Raisin wine	הגפן על הגפן	
Raisins	העץ על העץ	Some say they have insects.

FOOD	ברכה	NOTES
Raisins, chocolate coated	העץ בורא נפשות/על העץ	If outside is first sucked, then 2 ברכות.
Ramen noodles	מזונות על המחיה	Pre-cooked and edible.
Raspberry	------>	Should not be eaten, as it is nearly impossible to clean from insects.
Ratatouille	האדמה בורא נפשות	Made from eggplant.
Ravioli	מזונות על המחיה	
Raw dough	שהכל	Not דרך to be eaten.
Raw garlic	שהכל	Not דרך to be eaten.
Reese's Puffs cereal	שהכל בורא נפשות	Made from ground corn.
Red cabbage	האדמה בורא נפשות	
Rhubarb	האדמה בורא נפשות	
Rice	מזונות בורא נפשות	(בורא נפשות)
Rice cakes	האדמה בורא נפשות	Some say מזונות. (Either way it gets a בורא נפשות)
Rice Krispies cereal	מזונות בורא נפשות	Made from ground rice - בורא נפשות.
Rice Krispies treats	מזונות בורא נפשות	(בורא נפשות)
Rice kugel with raisins	מזונות בורא נפשות	(בורא נפשות)
Rock candy	שהכל בורא נפשות	
Rugelach	מזונות על המחיה	
Rum	שהכל	
Rum balls (cake)	מזונות על המחיה	
Rye bread	המוציא ברכת המזון	
Sabra/prickly pear	העץ בורא נפשות	
Salami	שהכל בורא נפשות	

FOOD	ברכה	NOTES
Salmon	שהכל בורא נפשות	
Salmon pate	שהכל בורא נפשות	
Salsa	------> בורא נפשות	If it is totally pureed, it's שהכל, but if there are pieces, make האדמה.
Salt	שהכל	
Sandwich	המוציא ברכת המזון	
Sardines	שהכל בורא נפשות	
Sauerkraut	האדמה בורא נפשות	
Scallion	שהכל בורא נפשות	Not the דרך to eat raw. Needs to be checked for insects.
Shawarma	שהכל בורא נפשות	
Scrambled eggs	שהכל בורא נפשות	
Seaweed/chips	שהכל בורא נפשות	Needs to be checked for insects.
Sesame chicken	שהכל בורא נפשות	
Sesame-seed candy	האדמה בורא נפשות	
Sesame seeds	האדמה בורא נפשות	
Sherbet	שהכל	No ברכה אחרונה since it is not consumed fast enough.
Shish kabob	האדמה and שהכל בורא נפשות	Since meat and vegetables are eaten separately.
Shnitzel	-------> בורא נפשות/על המחיה	If thick coating, מזונות; if thin coating, שהכל.
Shoko kid	שהכל בורא נפשות	
Shredded Wheat cereal	מזונות על המחיה	
Smirk bar	שהכל בורא נפשות	
Smoked salmon (lox)	שהכל בורא נפשות	
S'mores	מזונות על המחיה/ בורא נפשות	If eaten as one. If you eat marshmallows or chocolate separate, you need separate ברכות.

107

FOOD	ברכה	NOTES
Smoothie	-------> בורא נפשות/על העץ	If it is totally pureed with no pieces, it is שהכל. If there are still pieces, it is העץ if made with fruit.
Snackers	מזונות על המחיה	
Snap peas	האדמה בורא נפשות	
Snow peas	האדמה בורא נפשות	
Snapple	שהכל בורא נפשות	
Soda	שהכל בורא נפשות	
Soft or hardboiled egg	שהכל בורא נפשות	
Soup with noodles	-------> על המחיה---->	If mostly noodles, מזונות. If mostly soup, מזונות and שהכל. If a כזית of noodles is eaten within 4 minutes
Soup, instant	שהכל ------->	No הפסק since a רביעית is not consumed without a בורא נפשות.
Sour cream	שהכל בורא נפשות	
Sour sticks	שהכל בורא נפשות	
Soy nuts	האדמה בורא נפשות	They are made from soybeans that grow in the ground.
Soya mince	שהכל בורא נפשות	Made from soy flour.
Spaghetti	מזונות על המחיה	
Spanish rice	מזונות בורא נפשות	בורא נפשות
Special K cereal	מזונות על המחיה	Main ingredient is wheat flour.
Spelt cakes	האדמה ------->	It is puffed grain packed together. Some say to make מזונות, like rice cakes. See puffed wheat
Spinach	האדמה בורא נפשות	Needs to be checked for insects.
Split-pea soup	-------> בורא נפשות---->	If recognizable, האדמה; if fully dissolved, שהכל. If a כזית of split peas is eaten within 4 minutes.
Sponge cake	מזונות על המחיה	
Spring salad	-------> בורא נפשות	Vegetables w/ cottage cheese: if mostly cheese, make שהכל; if mainly vegetables, האדמה.

FOOD	ברכה	NOTES
Sprinkles	שהכל בורא נפשות	
Squash	האדמה בורא נפשות	
Starfruit	העץ בורא נפשות	
Strawberry	האדמה בורא נפשות	Needs to be checked for insects.
Strawberry shortcake	מזונות על המחיה	
String beans	האדמה בורא נפשות	
Strudel	מזונות על המחיה	
Stuffed cabbage – with meat	שהכל בורא נפשות	If meat is the רוב. (Unless you are eating it for the cabbage.)
Stuffed cabbage – with rice and meat	------> בורא נפשות	Make ברכה on whichever is רוב.
Stuffed pepper	------> בורא נפשות	If eaten separately, 2 ברכות; if not, make on רוב.
Stuffing	מזונות על המחיה	
Sugar/sugar cubes	שהכל בורא נפשות	
Sugar cane	שהכל	Because only flavor is eaten and not actual cane.
Sugar puffs	האדמה ------>	It is a puffed whole grain which is האדמה. For the ברכה אחרונה see buckwheat cakes.
Sunflower seeds	האדמה בורא נפשות	If in shell, needs to be checked for bugs! First make האדמה and eat seed before sucking salt on shell.
Sushi	------> בורא נפשות Tempura- על המחיה	ברכה follows whatever is the majority. If the rice is 51% then make a מזונות, if not, figure out the רוב. If unsure, make separate ברכות, preferably on other foods, but you can pick out from sushi. Deep-fried (tempura) is מזונות, as batter is flour.
Sweet potato	האדמה בורא נפשות	
Ta'ami bars	שהכל בורא נפשות	
Taco chips	שהכל בורא נפשות	
Takis chips	שהכל בורא נפשות	
Tam Tams	מזונות על המחיה	

FOOD	ברכה	NOTES
Tangerine	העץ בורא נפשות	
Tapioca pudding	שהכל בורא נפשות	
Tea	שהכל	No ברכה אחרונה since it is not consumed fast enough.
Tea loaf	מזונות על המחיה	
Techina	שהכל	
Tempura roll	מזונות על המחיה	
Terra chips	האדמה בורא נפשות	
Toast	המוציא ברכת המזון	
Toasted oats	מזונות על המחיה	
Toffee	שהכל בורא נפשות	
Tofu	שהכל בורא נפשות	Made from soy.
Tofutti	שהכל בורא נפשות	Soy ice cream.
Tomato	האדמה בורא נפשות	If grown in water, then שהכל.
Tomato juice	שהכל בורא נפשות	
Tomato soup	שהכל	No ברכה אחרונה since it is not consumed fast enough.
Tomato soup with rice	------> If lots of rice, then ----->בורא נפשות	Whatever the רוב is. Either a שהכל or a מזונות. If a כזית of rice is eaten within 4 minutes.
Tongue	שהכל בורא נפשות	
Tootie Fruities cereal	מזונות על המחיה	
Total cereal	מזונות על המחיה	
Tradition cup soup	מזונות על המחיה	Due to large amount of noodles, no שהכל is made.
Trail mix	------> See Muddy Buddies	If eaten one by one, you need separate ברכות. If eaten as a mixture, then it depends on what the mixture is made from. If there is Wheat Chex in it, it's automatically מזונות. If not, the ברכה is determined by the רוב.

FOOD	ברכה	NOTES
Trix cereal	שהכל בורא נפשות	Main ingredient is corn flour.
Tuna fish	שהכל בורא נפשות	
Tuna macaroni casserole	מזונות על המחיה	
Tuna steak	שהכל בורא נפשות	
Turkey	שהכל בורא נפשות	
Turnip	האדמה בורא נפשות	
Twizzlers	שהכל בורא נפשות	
Tylenol, flavored	שהכל	If taste is pleasant.
Tzimmis	האדמה בורא נפשות	Even if made with prunes or other fruit, they are בטל to the carrot.
Vanilla pudding	שהכל בורא נפשות	
Veal	שהכל בורא נפשות	
Vegetable salad	האדמה בורא נפשות	
Vegetable juices	שהכל בורא נפשות	Unless there are still pieces.
Vegetable soup	האדמה בורא נפשות – if a כזית of vegetables is eaten within 4 minutes.	Even when the soup is eaten alone, if the soup has a strong taste and the vegetables are the type that you cook and they were cooked to eat. If meat or chicken is added, ברכה is שהכל.
Vegetable soup with barley	מזונות על המחיה/בורא נפשות	If a כזית of barley or vegetables is eaten within 4 minutes.
Vegetables, mashed	------> בורא נפשות	If recognizable, האדמה; if not, שהכל.
Vegetarian burger	שהכל בורא נפשות	
Vegetarian schnitzel	שהכל בורא נפשות	
Veggie chips	שהכל בורא נפשות	
Viennese crunch	שהכל בורא נפשות	
Vitamins, unflavored	None	If the vitamins taste good, make a שהכל.
Wafers	מזונות על המחיה	

FOOD	ברכה	NOTES
Waffles	מזונות על המחיה	
Waldorf salad	העץ בורא נפשות	Apples are usually main ingredient.
Walnuts	העץ בורא נפשות	
Water	שהכל בורא נפשות	Unless you are not thirsty, and you are drinking for other purposes.
Watermelon	האדמה בורא נפשות	
Wheat cakes	האדמה ------>	It is made from puffed grain. Some say to make a מזונות like rice cakes. See puffed wheat.
Wheaties cereal	מזונות על המחיה	
Whipped cream	שהכל בורא נפשות	
Whiskey	שהכל	
White bread	המוציא ברכת המזון	
Whole-wheat bread	המוציא ברכת המזון	
Wine	הגפן על הגפן	
Winkies	שהכל בורא נפשות	
Wraps	------>	מחלוקת – Ask your local *rav*.
Yapchik	------> בורא נפשות	If it is made from potatoes and meat and you eat them both together, the ברכה is determined by the רוב. If you eat them separately, you need both ברכות.
Yerushalmi kugel	מזונות על המחיה	
Yodels	מזונות על המחיה	
Yogurt	שהכל (See ice cream)	Fruit is בטל.
Yogurt w/granola or fruit	------> (See ice cream/granola)	If the yogurt is the רוב, make a שהכל. If the granola or fruit is the רוב, make the ברכה on the granola or fruit.
Zetz	מזונות על המחיה	Contains wheat flour.
Zucchini	האדמה בורא נפשות	
Zucchini cake	מזונות על המחיה	

ברכות FOR VARIOUS OCCASIONS:

Upon seeing a non-Jewish King.	שנתן מכבודו לבשר ודם
Upon seeing a place where ניסים occurred for כלל ישראל.	שעשה ניסים לאבותינו במקום הזה
Upon seeing a place where one had personally experienced a נס.	שעשה לי נס במקום הזה
Upon hearing very good news shared by two or more people.	הטוב והמטיב
Upon hearing very bad news.	דיין האמת
Upon purchasing (or receiving as a present) a new home, furniture, clothes, jewelry, etc., that gives you great pleasure.	If it is for one person – שהחיינו If for two or more people - הטוב והמטיב
Upon recovering from a severe illness. (Some say to make this ברכה when flying overseas)	הגומל לחייבים טובות שגמלני כל טוב
Upon seeing the Atlantic or Pacific Ocean for the first time in 30 days.	שעשה את הים הגדול
Upon putting up a מזוזה.	לקבוע מזוזה
Upon toiveling כלים in a מקוה.	על טבילת כלי (כלים)
Upon seeing lightning and other astonishing natural phenomena. Shooting stars, earthquakes, really wild winds, the Alps, the Grand Canyon, the Rocky Mountains and Canadian Mountains, and very big bodies of water, including the Indian Ocean, Mediterranean, Red Sea, Niagara Falls (Canada side).	עושה מעשה בראשית
Upon hearing thunder, experiencing earthquakes, or tornadoes.	שכחו וגבורתו מלא עולם
Upon seeing a rainbow.	זוכר הברית ונאמן בבריתו וקים במאמרו
Upon wearing a new garment or jewelry of significant value that brings great שמחה to that person. Some make it when having a girl. (הטוב והמטיב for a boy.)	שהחיינו
Midget, hunchback, Siamese twins, one with extra limbs. Monkey, elephant. Only the first time.	משנה הבריות
Upon seeing the petals of a fruit tree in ניסן – as tree start to blossom.	שלא חיסר בעולמו כלום וברא בו בריות טובות ואילנות טובות ליהנות בהם בני אדם

113

Made in the USA
Middletown, DE
26 April 2022

64776584R00066